The Buc-ee's Phenomenon:

How a Gas Station Chain Achieved a Cult Following

Timothy Fay

While every precaution has been taken in the preparation of this book, the publisher assumes no responsibility for errors or omissions, or for damages resulting from the use of the information contained herein.

THE BUC-EE'S PHENOMENON: HOW A GAS STATION CHAIN ACHIEVED A CULT FOLLOWING

First edition. September 25, 2023.

Copyright © 2023 Timothy Fay.

ISBN: 979-8224704668

Written by Timothy Fay.

Gratitude:

Thank you to world traveler "Colleen B." for inspiring me to write this book. After a brief trip to Texas around the year 2019, she mentioned to me and other co-workers a "gigantic, super-clean gas station" called "Buc-ee's" — with a cult following. Hmmm. I thought about this for a day or two. I decided that I needed to "see what all the fuss was about." Tall tales from Texas? Or a real phenomenon? To find out... read on!

Introduction:

Why Write a Book About Buc-ee's?

Why did I write a book about Buc-ee's? To find out why people get excited about the mere mention of a convenience store chain: Buc-ee's.

Buc-ee's has grown from a "Texas thing" just a few years back to a retail powerhouse now found in seven states and counting. Buc-ee's now has stores in Alabama, Florida, Georgia, Kentucky, South Carolina, Tennessee, and of course: Texas. The chain plans to open stores soon in Colorado, Missouri, Oklahoma, and Wisconsin. Nearly everyone on their first visit to Buc-ee's is impressed with the size of the gas stations, the cleanliness of the stores (especially the bathrooms), the friendliness of the employees, and the tastiness of the freshly-made food. The cleverness of Buc-ee's marketing (old-school billboards "guiding" you to the next location with corny puns) is also a plus. Hence, the cult following.

Eighteen-wheelers are not allowed at Buc-ee's. But voracious fans are.

Join me in this non-Texan's (or perhaps "pre-Texan's") guide to the Buc-ee's phenomenon.

Chapter One

WHAT BUC-EE'S *IS*:

Buc-ee's *IS*: A retailer with a cult following.

The cleanliness of the locations, the size of the locations, the tastiness of the food, and the eye-catching souvenir selection are quite attractive for both new and repeat customers. The old-school feel of the Buc-ee's logo ... a grinning beaver wearing a ball cap, has added to the appeal. Buc-ee's could probably be described as what would happen if Disney got into the gas station/convenience store business.

Buc-ee's *IS*: A phenomenon.

Buc-ee's has experienced amazing growth since the year 2001, when the company began opening its gigantic "travel center" locations. Unlike many retailers, Buc-ee's opened new locations during the recent COVID pandemic. The largest Buc-ee's store is over 74,000 square feet: about the size of five or six medium-sized drug stores. Buc-ee's locations now stretch from Daytona Beach, Florida to Loveland, Colorado!

Buc-ee's *IS*: A place where you can hear an employee say on a walkie-talkie: "He's over at the kolache station."

You won't hear that at many other retailers. Kolaches are eastern-European fluffy-dough stuffed pastries. These treats can be filled with either sweet or savory stuffings. A favorite is a kolache stuffed with "dirty rice" and sausage. Some compare kolaches to the familiar "pig in a blanket" (croissant or other pastry stuffed with sausage). Kolaches were brought to Texas in the 1800s by Czech immigrants, and the treats have been popular in the Lone Star State ever since!

Buc-ee's *IS*: The record holder for the world's longest car wash.

Buc-ee's car washes are quite a production. But, when witnessed alongside the seemingly endless gas pumps, some hardly notice how massive the car washes are. The longest Buc-ee's car wash is about 30 miles from Houston at the Katy, Texas location. The car wash has a conveyor of 255 feet — nearly as long as a football field.

Buc-ee's *IS*: A godsend for road trippers.

Snacks, drinks, clean restrooms, fun souvenirs. A rest stop big enough for you to look around and stretch your legs for more than a minute or two ... and actually enjoy yourself (many say) while looking at the clever souvenirs. Plus a seemingly endless row of ice-bag freezers.

Buc-ee's *IS*: A money-making (private-sector) business that provides rest stops.

Buc-ee's could easily be thought of as a private-sector company that provides highway rest stops, which are normally provided by the state highway department or transportation department in most areas. It would be fun to know if highway departments plan the building and spacing of their rest areas "around" Buc-ee's locations.

Buc-ee's *IS*: A retailer where you can find the "Wall of Jerky."

Many Buc-ee's locations feature a "wall of jerky" with dozens of varieties of jerky (strips of dried, usually salted meat). Varieties of jerky for sale at some locations include Mesquite Peppered Beef Jerky, Cherry Maple Beef Jerky, and Ghost Pepper Beef Jerky! A favorite: "turkey jerky."

UP NEXT: What Buc-ee's is NOT.

We've told you some about what Buc-ee's IS. In the next episode, we'll talk about what Buc-ee's is NOT, which is probably even more revealing about the Buc-ee's story.

Chapter Two

WHAT BUC-EE'S IS *NOT*:

We've told you quite a bit about what Buc-ee's IS. Now we'll talk about what Buc-ee's is NOT, which says even more about the Buc-ee's story.

Buc-ee's is NOT publicly traded.

You can't buy shares of "Buc-ee's stock." The company is privately held by a small number of investors and the company is not publicly traded. Co-founder "Beaver" Arch Aplin in an interview with CBS News in the early 2020s said that not having to answer to shareholders gives the company more freedom to focus on the customer.

The privately-held status of Buc-ee's is a trait that Buc-ee's shares with another retailer with a very loyal following: Trader Joe's. Trader Joe's grocery store chain is also a privately held company.

Buc-ee's is NOT just a Gulf state phenomenon.

Just a few years ago, Buc-ee's had locations only in Texas, Alabama, and Florida (all states with Gulf of Mexico shorelines). The chain has since expanded to Georgia, Kentucky, South Carolina and Tennessee. Buc-ee's plans to open stores soon in Oklahoma and Wisconsin. The Wisconsin store will be the first store outside of an area that could be called the "Greater Southeast."

Buc-ee's is NOT what most would consider a grocery store or supermarket.

You can buy all sorts of snacks, sandwiches, beer, baked goods, and bar-becue at Buc-ee's. But, you probably wouldn't go to Buc-ee's to buy eggs, butter, flour, or fresh vegetables. In fact, Buc-ee's claims some of its locations are the world's largest convenience stores.

Buc-ee's is NOT a place where you can buy lottery tickets.

Again separating itself from the crowd of routine convenience stores, most Buc-ee's locations do not sell lottery tickets. This is in keeping with Buc-ee's mostly family-friendly and wholesome atmosphere. A question for the readers: Does this suggest an opportunity for a competitor to open a modest convenience-store selling lottery tickets across the street from a busy Buc-ee's location?

Buc-ee's is NOT a "general purpose" retailer like Target or Wal-mart.

You wouldn't go to Buc-ee's to buy a microwave oven or a bicycle. Perhaps instead, you probably *would* go there to buy all sorts of outdoor gear.

Buc-ee's is NOT a sit-down restaurant. Not even close.

All the food at most large Buc-ee's locations is "to go." This results in some makeshift arrangements for travelers. Some eat Buc-ee's sandwiches in their vehicles. Some eat standing around their cars in the parking lot, in a "quickie" tailgate arrangement. Some eat standing around in the store (apparently frowned upon by Buc-ee's employees).

Buc-ee's is NOT a place where you can sit down, even when not dining.

Buc-ee's motto might as well be "moving right along." There are no chairs inside the store. There are no benches near the entrance. In fact, lawn chairs and beach chairs for sale at Buc-ee's have signs warning patrons that the items are for display and that customers should seek "employee assistance" if needed. In other words, "Don't sit down!"

Some speculate that this is because Buc-ee's is in the gas station business, not the sit-down restaurant business. Another consideration is that some customers might park their car at the gas pumps and then go inside Buc-ee's and enjoy a leisurely meal — *if* Buc-ee's was a sit-down restaurant. It appears that Buc-ee's is preempting this behavior—which would tie up the gas pumps.

Of course there is one place where you can sit down at Buc-ee's — in the ultra clean restroom stalls.

Buc-ee's is NOT a place that sells propane… or propane accessories.

Hank Hill, the main character of the Texas-based TV comedy *King of the Hill,* would be happy to know this. Less competition for his employer "Strickland Propane" in the popular animated TV comedy series.

The Buc-ee's website does not explain why the company does not sell propane. However, many competitor convenience-stores do sell propane.

Buc-ee's is NOT a truck stop.

Eighteen-wheelers (large tractor-trailer truck combos) are not allowed at Buc-ee's as customer conveyances. This policy probably adds to the appeal for "four-wheeler" customers.

This policy has sparked a nearly inevitable trend: drivers of eighteen-wheelers simply park across the street (often an access road) and then stroll to Buc-ee's for their favorite barbecue and "energy drinks." And they probably also use the restroom while they're there.

Buc-ee's does NOT have a listed phone number for most of its locations.

Long ago, Buc-ee's found that customers became irritated when employees answered the phone rather than waiting on in-store clients. Therefore, Buc-ee's encourages clients to refer to its website for info.

Buc-ee's does feature nostalgia-themed gifts in its souvenir and apparel section, but Buc-ee's does NOT overwhelm customers with the nostalgia theme.

Buc-ee's does not overwhelm — or turn on the "nostalgia fire hose." This differentiates Buc-ee's from the popular restaurant-chain Cracker Barrel. The gift section at Cracker Barrel seems to induce nostalgia overload.

FAST FACTS ABOUT BUC-EE'S

● Buc-ee's was founded in 1982 by Don Wasek and Arch "Beaver" Aplin III. Aplin often appears at the "grand openings" of new Buc-ee's locations, wearing a Western-style hat.

● Some Buc-ee's locations have up to 120 fueling positions (pumps) and hundreds of parking spaces. The recently opened Sevierville, Tennessee Buc-ee's location reportedly has 128 fueling positions.

● Buc-ee's is well known for these homemade items: fudge, sandwiches, a wide variety of baked goods, burritos, brisket, and roasted nuts.

● Buc-ee's has headquarters in Lake Jackson, Texas, about 50 miles south of downtown Houston.

Chapter Three

———

HOW BUC-EE'S BUILT A

CULT FOLLOWING:

CULT BUILDER #1:

CONVENIENCE

Buc-ee's beats many competitors — convenience stores — at their own game regarding ease of use and customer friendliness. And the convenience starts before you even get to Buc-ee's.

To demonstrate this, I will retrace my "steps" from several visits to the Katy, Texas, location.

Buc-ee's often has a "breadcrumb" trail of billboards leading to its stores — like a homing beacon — keeping you posted on how long you need to "hold it." The Buc-ee's beacon system.

The travel center locations have towering signs — featuring Buc-ee the beaver — visible for motorists traveling in nearly any direction.

Most Buc-ee's locations since the early 2000s are on nearly gigantic lots with plentiful parking. Working with local highway departments, Buc-ee's has done its darndest to allow easy "in and out" of its locations. Because of the popularity of Buc-ee's, one-lane exit ramps do back up sometimes—an "exit jam." Here, Buc-ee's is sometimes a victim of its own success.

CONVENIENT HOURS:

Buc-ee's travel centers are open 24 hours. It's hard to beat that for convenience, especially if you like to get an early start or drive through the night.

CONVENIENT REFUELING:

Let's look at the gas pumps. Buc-ee's has over 100 fueling stations at many of its travel centers! The gas pump area is very spacious, and quite convenient both for someone in a Mazda Miata or for someone in a Ford Expedition. And Buc-ee's provides an array of "fuels." At many locations, Buc-ee's provides several varieties of gasoline, diesel, and Tesla-branded "Supercharger" electric charging stations.

Car washes and rather pleasant grassy "pet relief stations" add to the convenience at the larger locations.

As the customer walks from the pumps to the store's interior, he or she passes myriad ice chests filled with super cheap bags of ice. You will never have to wait in line behind someone at the ice chest.

Once inside the store, the convenience continues.

Buc-ee's has very wide aisles. Too bad this seems like a novel concept in retail these days. Customers will notice that, in most cases, they can walk from the store entrance to the restroom (near the back of the store), walking only through very wide aisles and not dodging the irritating "merchandiser" displays that *nearly* block grocery-store aisles.

***VERY* CONVENIENT RESTROOMS:**

Which brings us to the restrooms. It's hard to imagine anything more convenient than the spacious, clean restrooms. Some locations have over 80 stalls. Cleaning attendants are almost always on duty when the restrooms are busy.

The restrooms are near the back of the store via wide aisles, but not too far back. There's little or no dodging someone opening a door to the beer cooler on the way to the restrooms.

Fill up your tank, empty your bladder. A "rest stop," indeed.

CONVENIENT FOOD AND DRINK:

Buc-ee's food options are incredibly convenient if you're in a hurry. Freshly made hot sandwiches, tacos, etc., await you "in the hopper" at the barbecue pit. Custom sandwiches are available via the Buc-ee's kiosk system inside the store.

If you want healthy — or at least "healthier" options — Buc-ee's has cups of freshly chopped fruit (such as pineapples) available in the coolers. Yogurt options also abound.

The drink options are also very convenient. The "soda wall" and the "coffee wall" at most stores have nearly countless self-serve dispensers, greatly reducing the odds of waiting behind a fellow customer.

Then there's Buc-ee's snacks—an impressive variety of chips, crackers, and cheese. "Protein packs" include meats, cheese, and crackers. Much needed supplies for road tripping. Nearly all of Buc-ee's food selections are ready to eat—no cooking required.

CONVENIENT CHECKOUT:

Buc-ee's stores sometimes have over 20 cash registers for checkout. The *Washington Post* recently noted that the New Braunfels, Texas Buc-ee's has over 31 cash registers... at a convenience store!

CONVENIENTLY AVOIDING "IN-APP PURCHASES" AND "MEMBER PRICING" BALONEY:

A very appealing—and convenient—way of doing business for most customers in a hurry. Buc-ee's does not push customers to "download the app." There's no phony baloney "member price" and "schmuck price." Just one price. Nothing is worse than waiting at a Kroger behind a fellow customer at the checkout complaining that he didn't get the "member price."

There is one way to get a discount at Buc-ee's. A subset of customers can get a five percent discount at Buc-ee's when using a TDECU credit union Visa-branded credit card. Only TDECU credit union members are eligible to apply for the card. TDECU began as a credit union for Dow Chemical employees based in East Texas—hence the acronym. It's a bit complicated, but most Texas residents can now apply for TDECU membership. If you're interested, find out more at tdecu.org.

THE "NOT-SO" CONVENIENT:

For some —perhaps many— not everything is convenient at Buc-ee's. Some dining tables *would be* very convenient—or how about some picnic tables outside? And how about some pickleball courts? Just kidding about the pickleball. Before we're too hard on Buc-ee's about the lack of in-store dining, we probably should note that the lack of dining tables is not just a Buc-ee's trend. It seems that restaurant chain locations that open new locations have ever smaller dining rooms. And some hotels no longer have waiting benches at the entrance.

Lugging your hot meal out to your car, especially on a cold rainy day, is not fun. Inevitably, your car will get messier with every stop at Buc-ee's. But even here, Buc-ee's has some "semi-convenient" solutions. Many locations sell dining trays with cup holders for dining in your car. The kid's trays are shaped to conform to the kid's "thigh-tops," creating a more stable "tabletop."

And Buc-ee's locations with car washes do feature self-serve vacuum cleaners. It's not a bad idea to do a quick vacuuming—especially if you get the kids involved in the "teamwork."

To summarize, Buc-ee's is *very convenient*. Though primarily convenient if you're in a hurry. It is not convenient if you want to relax inside the store rather than dine in your car.

CULT BUILDER #2:

ATTRACTIVE PRICES

A "nice price" is one of the attractions that Buc-ee's uses to create a devoted following—a nice price on gas, a nice price on ice, and on many other items.

Observers note that Buc-ee's gasoline is typically about thirty cents a gallon cheaper than many competitors. Customers who purchase a car wash (when refueling) enjoy an even lower gas price at many locations.

Many food options at Buc-ee's are also attractively priced — considering the convenience and the freshness of Buc-ee's food options.

Buc-ee's dining options, such as brisket sandwiches, tacos, and burritos, are in many cases only slightly higher in price than fast-food competitors but are higher in quality and freshness, most would agree.

Buc-ee's does have items that are not particularly cheap. These include souvenirs, T-shirts, and jerky. Most folks probably expect a bit of a markup regarding souvenirs and T-shirts. And souvenirs are not exactly necessities... for most folks. The jerky — such as beef and turkey jerky — is challenging to make, is low on artificial preservatives, and is a form of "concentrated," convenient protein. Though not cheap, Buc-ee's jerky doesn't appear much more expensive than other high-quality producers. Some fresh jerky varieties are available for around $29.95 per pound. Sounds expensive to many customers. But considering its freshness, yumminess, and convenience, devoted customers buy thousands of pounds of jerky.

CULT BUILDER #3:

YUMMINESS

I hope the reader's not too hungry—or on a diet—at the moment. Buc-ee's has a nearly endless array of snacks and treats, plus a rather solid selection of choices that most (most Texans, anyway) would call "entrees," such as barbecue, burritos, and tacos.

Some of the "stars" of the show are the fresh-cooked brisket, kolaches (a central European pastry), fresh-roasted nuts, fresh fudge, and countless drink options. Buc-ee's gets your attention food-wise. You smell the nearly irresistible barbecue and roasting nuts when you enter the store. The fudge station is a bit of a feast for the eyes, with selections including "birthday cake," "tiger stripe," and "blueberry cheesecake." Damnit!

An incessant favorite is Buc-ee's fresh ly-made banana pudding with vanilla wafers, available in "to-go" cups in coolers near the store's center.

Did someone mention Beaver Nuggets? This sweet, crunchy snack is a hallmark of Buc-ee's. Beaver Nuggets are made of corn flour and are somewhat akin to "Corn Pops," with a bit more of a caramelized shell. Just don't let your Mom catch you buying Beaver Nuggets—unless she also likes them.

———————

Kolaches are a Buc-ee's fan favorite. These are fluffy-dough stuffed pastries filled with either sweet or savory stuffings. Kolaches stuffed with "dirty rice" and sausage are a popular choice. Some compare kolaches to the familiar "pig in a blanket" (croissant or other pastry stuffed with sausage). Kolaches were brought to Texas in the 1800s by Czech immigrants.

If you just want snacks, Buc-ee's has many snacks you'd find in a grocery store. But why buy a cellophane bag of Lay's potato chips when you can buy Buc-ee's fresh homemade potato chips? Why buy a jar of Planters peanuts when you can buy Buc-ee's freshly roasted, glazed pecans in an old-school wax-paper cone?

YUMMY DRINK:

All that food requires something to "wash it down," and Buc-ee's is up to the challenge. First, there's the soda fountain. Some Buc-ee's locations have 64 choices in the self-serve soda fountain!

Sweet tea is a perennial favorite... it can be sucked down by the gallon. But try not to do that. Otherwise, you will need to stop at the *next* Buc-ee's on your road trip. And yes, it does appear that Buc-ee's copious drink selections and clean restrooms together form some sort of "guerrilla" marketing strategy.

And... don't worry, Buc-ee's has a wide selection of beer and wine available in the "grocery section," including six packs and bottles of wine. No alcohol consumption is permitted in the stores.

CULT BUILDER #4:

CLEANLINESS

For many years, Buc-ee's has taken pride in the tidiness of its locations, especially its bathrooms. This isn't just hype. Many customers will attest that the bathrooms are quite clean. The New Braunfels, Texas Buc-ee's store in 2012 won the "America's Best Restroom Award" from Cintas, a workplace supply company. The website bestrestroom.com, produced by Cintas, claimed that the New Braunfels store's bathrooms "flushed the competition when it comes to clean" back in 2012. Considering that the New Braunfels location (not far from San Antonio) had 83 bathroom stalls at the time, keeping the bathrooms clean is a rather impressive feat.

Usually, when visiting Buc-ee's, you will notice attendants busily cleaning the restrooms — while you use the restroom. Cleaning the restrooms at Buc-ee's is not a "once or twice a day" event. It's a constant undertaking. As many insiders have noted, "retail is detail!"

I've made several visits to Buc-ee's locations both in Texas and Colorado. The restrooms and retail areas were quite clean on all my visits. I was super impressed with the tidiness of the endless soda fountains and coffee stations. Careless customers at many rest stops slop around coffee, soda, sugar, and cream. But Buc-ee's manages to keep the areas exceptionally clean. Indeed, it appears that this cleanliness is a bit "contagious." For instance, customers at the coffee stations may be a bit more careful than customers at a typical convenience store — partially preventing messiness in the first place.

On most visits to Buc-ee's, clients will notice that the tidiness begins in the parking lot and gas pump area. Rarely will you see a serious litter problem in the parking lot. And it appears that gas pumps are regularly wiped down. You will see a refreshing change from the grimy gas pumps at some competitors.

CULT BUILDER #5:

FUN!

───

In terms of Buc-ee's cult-building attributes, we've saved the best for last... fun! How many other places serve "Sausage on a Stick"? This treat resembles a corn dog but features a sausage wrapped in a tortilla... on a stick.

The fun starts in the parking lot with a gigantic Buc-ee the beaver sign. Plus, there's a bronze statue of Buc-ee near the entrance of most Buc-ee's travel center locations. A photo opp for road trippers!

Next is the "Let's Go Nuts!" station, with its mesmerizing turntable of slowly roasting glazed nuts—a feast for the nose, the eyes, and well... for nearly all of the senses.

Then, there is the souvenir and apparel section. Even hard-boiled folks who wouldn't usually stroll the souvenir section seem to lighten up at Buc-ee's. Fun items include turquoise-clad cow skulls, Buc-ee Beaver "onesie" costumes, Buc-ee's branded boxer shorts, Buc-ee Beaver bobbleheads, old-school "billboard-style" fridge magnets, and Buc-ee's dog sweaters.

Elevating Buc-ee's from "just a store" to an experience, Buc-ee's locations have features you associate with tourist attractions. These include:

- A trail of billboards—reminiscent of old-school roadside attractions—spaced every 30 miles or so, guiding you to the store—and building excitement for the kids!

• Car wash conveyors at some locations (including Katy, Texas) have light show features. The car wash is akin to a low-key amusement ride. Clean fun.

• Penny presses, usually found at tourist attractions. Don't forget your quarters. And a penny.

• Foods you often find at amusement parks and tourist spots, including cotton candy, freshly-made fudge, fresh-roasted nuts, saltwater taffy, "Dippin Dots" ice cream, and "nostalgia-inducing" candy selections.

Other fun-inducing features include:

• The "Buc-ee's Truck." An old-school truck near the center of large Buc-ee's locations that serves as a sort of "guidepost" within the store.

• Samples! Who can argue with that? Buc-ee's sometimes will proactively offer roasted nuts samples at a "sample station" near the cash registers. Customers are encouraged to ask for samples at the "Let's Go Nuts!" station and the "Jerky Deli." But please don't be a "sample hog."

• Art in the restrooms, such as framed paintings and prints. A nice touch. And yes, the art is for sale.

• A nearly endless selection of outdoor and barbecue gear brings out the sportsman/sportswoman in just about anyone. These include collapsible "deer stands," "deer corn," crawdad boilers, fire pits, and so on. An appliance store in some respects but an "outdoor appliance store." Browsing or buying, this stuff is fun. Dropping hints to spouses about what a "nice Christmas present" that grill would make... is permitted. Where else can city folks check out crawdad boilers and deer feeders? After a Buc-ee's visit, city folks might not go back to the city!

Then there are the not-so-little things, including cheerful and attentive employees. Buc-ee's employees greet customers when shoppers enter the stores. Barbecue pit employees cheerfully shout, "Fresh Brisket on the board," when a new batch comes out of the oven.

It's reported that employees in customer-facing areas are not allowed to stare at their smartphones while on duty. After several visits to Buc-ee's locations in Colorado and Texas, I haven't seen any employees on duty staring at their smartphones.

It's the fun that makes Buc-ee's a destination. And "fun" is what elevates Buc-ee's from a well-run convenience store to a place with a cult following.

By now you've probably noticed the last two "cult-building" qualities are cleanliness and fun. That's not a coincidence. Good, "clean fun" makes Buc-ee's super popular for kids, parents, and everyone else.

More than a few have compared Buc-ee's to Disney's Magic Kingdom. Dare we call Buc-ee's the *"Magic Rest Stop"*?

Chapter Four

Understanding Buc-ee's —

The "Buctionary":

A Dictionary

Guide to Buc-ee's, From A to Z

In order to best understand the Buc-ee's phenomenon, let's look at key facts and players in the Buc-ee's story. Here is a "Buc-ee's Dictionary" with all you want to know about the popular chain.

The "Buc-ee's Dictionary" is not authorized nor endorsed by Buc-ee's.

- A -

Alabama: Buc-ee's chose Alabama for its first location outside of Texas. As of mid-2023, Buc-ee's had four locations in the "Heart of Dixie" (Alabama).

Alabama locations include **Loxley** (sometimes referred to as the **"Robertsdale"** location). This was the first location outside of Texas. The Loxley store is along Interstate 10, which skirts the Gulf Coast. The Loxley location is next to the intersection of I-10 and the Baldwin Beach Express highway, about 30 miles north of Gulf Shores.

Buc-ee's also has a store in **Leeds, Alabama,** which is considered a suburb of **Birmingham.** The Leeds location is along Interstate 20, about 20 miles east of downtown Birmingham.

In late 2021, Buc-ee's broke ground for a third Alabama location near **Auburn**. The Auburn location opened in April, 2023. The **Athens, Alabama** location also opened in 2023.

Arch "Beaver" Aplin III: Buc-ee's was founded in 1982 by Arch "Beaver" Aplin III. Aplin was involved in the construction business when he noticed a parcel of land for sale near an intersection in **Lake Jackson, Texas.** Aplin thought the parcel was a great location for a convenience store and purchased the property, opening the first Buc-ee's there. Lake Jackson, about 50 miles south of downtown **Houston,** is the site of Buc-ee's headquarters. These days, Aplin often appears at the "grand openings" of Buc-ee's locations, wearing a Western-style hat.

Backstory, or "buc-story": The backstory of Buc-ee's. The firm started as a small chain of neighborhood convenience stores mostly south of the Houston, Texas area in the early 1980s. During the 1980s and 1990s, most Buc-ee's locations were not extraordinarily large. Beginning about 2003, the firm started opening its "travel centers": gigantic gas stations. Indeed, some of Buc-ee's locations are the largest gas stations in the world. These mega-centers are rarely located near a large downtown or even near the bulk of the suburbs of any major cities.

'Bago: Recreational Vehicle enthusiast's slang for "Winnebago." Buc-ee's is ever-popular with RVers — for rest stops — but *not* for overnight camping. Indeed, some locations seem to be a magnet for RVers. For instance, the Katy, Texas Buc-ee's location has two large RV sales and supply locations (not owned by Buc-ee's) nearby.

"Balance": Buc-ee's appears to have struck a balance in terms of maintaining a family-friendly atmosphere. Buc-ee's does sell alcohol such as beer and wine. But Buc-ee's locations do not appear to have an emphasis on alcohol sales. Unlike many mainstream supermarket chains, Buc-ee's does not display beer and wine on the "end stop" of nearly every aisle in the store. Beer and wine is simply found in the... beer and wine section.

Further instilling a decent balance, Buc-ee's does sell T-shirts with suggestive slogans. But the chain does *not* sell T-shirts with *raunchy* slogans.

Again separating itself from the crowd of routine convenience stores, most Buc-ee's locations do not sell lottery tickets. This is in keeping with Buc-ee's mostly family-friendly and wholesome atmosphere.

Barbecue: Buc-ee's features an array of barbecue eating options, including brisket and barbecue pork. Buc-ee's barbeque sauce is also "bottled up" and is — of course — available for purchase.

Barbecue equipment: At larger Buc-ee's locations, customers can view a wide variety of smokers, barbeque pits, and other barbeque gear available for purchase on the sidewalk near the entrance. Possibly a form of advertising... getting you primed for ordering barbecue, brisket, and other items once you enter the store. The placement of the barbecue equipment for sale on the sidewalk is possibly also an effort to deter customers from having impromptu picnics on the sidewalk after ordering their Buc-ee's take-out food.

baskets: Shopping baskets are available to hold the many items you might purchase in a Buc-ee's. It's probably not often that clients want a shopping basket at a gas station — except at Buc-ee's. Some clients even opt for shopping carts. *See also:* **Buc-ee's buggies.**

bathrooms, ultra-clean: Buc-ee's advertises its ultra-clean bathrooms and most folks agree that the chain does a very good job of keeping the restrooms clean. Perhaps part of the reason for this is because there are simply so many stalls and urinals at Buc-ee's locations. Therefore, any one particular bathroom stall doesn't get dirty as quickly. The other reason the bathrooms are clean is: constant cleaning by dedicated employees. df

bathroom designer: Buc-ee's founder "Beaver" Aplin reports that he has designed the bathrooms at many Buc-ee's locations. Aplin does have a background in construction and building design. In fact some customers are so happy with the design of the restrooms at Buc-ee's that they've asked for the design plans.

battery chargers: Many Buc-ee's locations have electric vehicle charging stations — especially "Tesla Supercharger" stations — in addition to the myriad gasoline pumps. An example is the Florence, South Carolina location. It appears that most of the travel centers that have opened since about the year 2021 have charging stations on the Buc-ee's site — or on an adjacent property. It's hard to imagine a more inviting rest stop to visit while your vehicle charges for 20 minutes or so.

"Battleground State": Florida has become a bit of a battleground state — two convenience store chains with cult (or near-cult) followings have expanded from their home states and now compete in Florida. In addition, Florida-based Busy Bee convenience stores appear to have a devoted following. Philadelphia-based Wawa, Inc. now has many stores in Florida. Wawa's fresh food selection — especially its fresh sandwiches — are a hit with customers, many of whom are multi-generation Wawa consumers. Buc-ee's now has two large "travel center" locations in Florida: Daytona Beach and St. Augustine, in competition with Wawa. Busy Bee has several large gas station/convenience store locations in north Florida — competing with Wawa and Buc-ee's. In addition, yet another convenience store chain is entering the Florida market: Parker's. No shortage of competition.

Bayous: Buc-ee's got its start in the area south of Houston, Texas. "Creeks" and other waterways in the Houston area are sometimes referred to as "bayous", including Buffalo Bayou and White Oak Bayou. Not surprisingly, Buc-ee's devotes a sizable portion of its retail space to fishing gear. An eye-opening item for sale at many Buc-ee's locations: in the outdoor gear and barbecue equipment aisles, customers can find crawdad boilers.

B.B.: Before Buc-ee's. An area where a Buc-ee' location has opened has two eras: "Before Buc-ee's" ... and "After Buc-ee's."

B.C.: Before Coffee. An awkward time of the day when someone hasn't yet properly caffeinated himself or herself. Most Buc-ee's locations have large coffee stations with many selections of freshly-brewed coffee, sweeteners, and creams. Unlike self-serve coffee stations at many other establishments, the coffee stations at Buc-ee's are kept very clean.

"Be kind.": An admirable slogan of Buc-ee's management and employees.

Beach-area locations: Buc-ee's has mega travel centers in, near, — *or on the exit leading to* — several beach destinations, listed below. These locations are near beaches in four states. Here are some Buc-ee's locations near, or on the exit leading to beach destinations — we've listed the stores generally from west to east, reflecting the direction of Buc-ee's expansion.

- **Texas City, Texas.** The Buc-ee's store in Texas City is about 20 miles from the nearest beaches in Galveston.

- **Loxley, Alabama.** The Buc-ee's location in Loxley is along Interstate 10. The Loxley Buc-ee's store is about 30 miles from the nearest beaches in Gulf Shores.

- **Daytona Beach, Florida.** The Buc-ee's location is in Daytona Beach.

- **St. Augustine, Florida.** The Buc-ee's store is in St. Augustine.

- **Florence, South Carolina.** The Buc-ee's store in Florence is along Interstate 95 and is near the I-95 exit used by many when driving to Myrtle Beach. The Florence store is about 67 miles from the nearest beaches in Myrtle Beach — but is probably an ideal rest stop for those headed to the beach.

Now your two favorite things together: the beach, and Buc-ee's. Indeed Buc-ee's is a very "convenient" stop on the way to the beach — to load up on ice, snacks, drinks, beach floats, and sunblock.

Example: *TV reporter— "Looks like you folks near the coast now have some Buc-ee's locations in your neighborhood. Lucky beaches!"*

"Beaver believers": Nickname for "cult followers" of Buc-ee's — of which there are many — especially in the Lone Star State. The cult following appears to be spreading rapidly in other areas of the country as Buc-ee's expands.

Beaver bikinis: Yes, readers, Buc-ee's has Buc-ee's branded bikinis complete with the "beaver logo" on the bikini bottoms.

Beaver boxers: Boxer shorts featuring the Buc-ee's beaver logo are available at many Buc-ee's locations.

"Beaver Bucks": Buc-ee's gift cards. Customers can buy the gift cards on buc-ees.com, and then cheerfully spend the "gift cards" on brisket, beer and gear at Buc-ee's. According to the company's website, the gift cards are only available online — at buc-ees.com.

"Beaver Buddies": Buc-ee's brand of animal crackers. In keeping with a retro old-school look, the cracker box depicts an old-fashioned circus wagon on all sides. Another offering which adds to the family-friendly appeal of Buc-ee's.

"Beaver Fever": "Pumped-up" excitement during a visit to Buc-ee's. Especially someone's first visit — or a visit to the grand opening of a Buc-ee's location. A riff on "Bieber Fever": swooning over singer Justin Bieber.

"Beaver Freezers": Frozen treats available at many Buc-ee's locations, similar to popsicles. They are called "freezer pops" by many. Flavors include pineapple, "blue-berry cheesecake," and "birthday cake."

Beaver Nuggets: Sweet, crunchy snack, which is a signature product of Buc-ee's. Many consider buying Beaver Nuggets a "must" when visiting Texas. Beaver Nuggets are made of corn flour and are *somewhat* similar to Kellogg's Corn Pops breakfast cereal. However, Beaver Nuggets are generally more caramelized than Corn Pops. If you need to lose a few pounds (like most folks), *please* don't tell your doctor you like Beaver Nuggets.

Beer: Sales of fermented alcoholic beverages are quite important at Buc-ee's, as beer sales are just about anywhere in Texas — or any "warm" place. Please remember that this chain was started in Texas. And while you're remembering things, please "Remember the Alamo."

"Beer season": Slogan on more than a few T-shirts for sale at Buc-ee's. Rather than proclaiming it's "deer season," the shirts proclaim it is now — and always will be — beer season.

"beer thirty": Beer-drinking time. Many a Buc-ee's patron has purchased beer just before "beer thirty." The exact timing of "beer thirty" varies from customer to customer. Most — though not all — say "beer thirty" occurs shortly after finishing work for the day.

Benefits: Buc-ee's employees enjoy benefits including health care, a retirement fund, and paid vacation. Not bad at all for a gas station — though many will say that Buc-ee's is much more than a gas station.

Bento Boxes: As many Americans know, "bentos" are Japanese-style carefully-prepared box lunches. These are often sold at train stations in Japan. Often a feast for the eyes, bento boxes will contain several rectangular "compartments" within the box, often containing several different colorful and tempting food items within the compartments. Buc-ee's "Fudge Variety Pack", packed up neatly in a rectangular box, is a sort of bento box... for those who want to conveniently inhale calories.

BFGT: Buy Four, Get Two (Free). Sales pitch used for Buc-ee's freshly made fudge on signs displayed at the "fudge station." Similar to "BOGO" — Buy One, Get One — except much more calorie-inducing.

Bibs: Bibs for babies. Yes, Buc-ee's does have Buc-ee's branded baby bibs with a beaver logo. In fact, Buc-ee's has a fairly extensive selection of baby clothes for sale at many locations.

(The) "Big D": 1. Divorce. **2.** Dallas, Texas. Buc-ee's does have several locations in the greater Dallas area. For instance, the **Terrell, Texas** location is along Interstate 20, about 27 miles east of downtown Dallas.

Big brass belt buckles: Buc-ee's does sell Western-style belt buckles — traditionally a "trophy" of rodeo champions. This brings up a perennial question:

What are the three biggest lies in Texas?

1. "I won this belt buckle in a rodeo."
2. "The truck is paid for."
3. "I only go to Buc-ee's for my kids."

"Bigger in Texas": The **New Braunfels, Texas** location *was* the largest Buc-ee's location until the summer of 2023. New Braunfels is about 30 miles northeast coming up from San Antonio. Or, as singer George Strait says — "San An-tone." The store was surpassed in 2023 by the **Sevierville, Tennessee** location

Bigger in Texas (not): Buc-ee's recently opened its biggest store ever — in Tennessee. Buc-ee's claims the Sevierville, Tennessee store is in a "gateway" location for vacationers heading to the Smoky Mountains — a long way from the plains of East Texas, where Buc-ee's began.

Are we reaching the point when we can no longer say that the company is primarily a Texas phenomenon? A real concern for many Texans. For instance, some say that the popular Texas-based "Whataburger" hamburger chain lost its mojo when it expanded far and wide beyond the Lone Star State. Damnit!

Billboards: These large outdoor signs are a hallmark of Buc-ee's marketing These signs feature corny yuk-yuk slogans. Reminiscent of old-school "roadside attractions," the billboards appear strategically as you approach a Buc-ee's location. Some of the signs have slogans such as:

"Next location 41 miles. You can hold it."

"There are two reasons to stop here. Reason Number 1, and Reason Number 2."

Finally! A place where dads get to make a living off of their "dad jokes." Do the jokes on the billboards reach the level of side splitting humor — and therefore a "hazard" for motorists? Welllll... not yet.

Birthday-cake flavored freezer pops: Buc-ee's now features this flavor of "freezer pops." Buc-ee's brand is **Beaver Freezers.** There seems to be something going on with aquatic, furry critters and the "naming" of frozen treats: "Otter Pops," "Beaver Freezers." We'll stop right there.

Bladders: One of the top reasons for stopping at Buc-ee's — to relieve your bladder. Buc-ee's has taken pride in its ultra-clean restrooms for many years.

Bladder "range": The distance someone can drive without needing to use the restroom. Some have noted their bladder's "range" is about 300 miles—about the same as their electric car's "battery range."

Blue Creme soda: Considered a specialty of Buc-ee's. Buc-ee's branding does include the "creme" spelling, rather than the "standard" "cream" spelling. Some describe the flavor as something akin to bubblegum.

Bluegrass Buc-ee's: "Kentucky Buc-ee's." Buc-ee's recently opened its first store in the Bluegrass State in **Richmond, Kentucky.** The store is along Interstate 75 and is about 30 miles south of **Lexington, Kentucky.** If Lexington is not a sufficient landmark for you, we will add that the Richmond, Kentucky location is about 110 miles south of **Cincinnati, Ohio.**

"Bobtailing": Driving the "tractor" of an (otherwise) "18-wheeler" rig, but without the trailer. The "tractor" or "semi" in many common arrangements has ten wheels, while the trailer has eight wheels. "Eighteen-wheeler" truck rigs are not permitted as customer conveyances at Buc-ee's. However, "bobtailing" is a tactic some truckers use in an attempt to be able to visit Buc-ee's. However, *even this tactic* is not permitted in at least some Buc-ee's locations. Needless to say, some truckers (perhaps many) don't appreciate that they are effectively not permitted at Buc-ee's — at least not while driving a big rig.

"Boon-docking": Camping (or living) in an RV in a remote location with no utility "hookups."

"Boot ranches": Texas-based retailers of Western-style boots, often featuring a large selection. For example, Gomez Boot Ranch is about two miles from the **Katy, Texas** Buc-ee's location along Interstate 10.

"Born-again Texan": A person who, once they've moved to Texas, completely adopts a Texas-oriented Lifestyle. Such a person embraces: Buc-ee's, boots, barbecue, and Shiner Bock beer.

Boudin: 1.: A popular style of kolache with a "filling" often containing Louisiana-style "dirty rice" and Boudin sausage. Buc-ee's Boudin kolaches are quite tasty, in the opinion of your friendly neighborhood author. **2.:** A very popular bakery in the San Francisco area, which is one of the oldest businesses in the Bay Area. Boudin Bakery is renowned for its "ancestral" sourdough bread. Come to think of it, Boudin sausage and Boudin Bakery sourdough bread might go quite well together.

Bowl games: Many Buc-ee's locations are "on the way" to, or are nearby many college football "bowl game" locations in the Southern United States — and are an ideal location for buying food, drinks, gas, and of course, *b*eer. For instance, the Gator Bowl is held annually in Jacksonville, Florida. So why not stop off at the Daytona Beach — or St. Augustine, Florida — locations before or after the game? Or during the game, if you'e not a football person.

Boxers: "Buc-ee's Boxers." Buc-ee's branded men's underwear is available for purchase at many locations.

"Bracketing" (cities): A pattern Buc-ee's patrons will notice. Buc-ee's seems to "bracket" or "bookend" cities with huge "travel centers" about 40 or 50 miles on either side of downtown.

Brassieres: Old school term for bras. Buc-ee's, of course, sells Buc-ee's-branded brassieres.

Brazoria location: One of Buc-ee's older, smaller stores, the Brazoria, Texas, location is about 60 miles south-southwest of downtown Houston. Though a smaller location, the store does feature a wide selection of freshly-prepared food — like nearly all of Buc-ee's locations. A sought after item: Buc-ee's Brazoria brassieres.

"brekkie briskie": Brisket for breakfast, which is available at Buc-ee's in sandwiches, biscuits, and burritos.

"Brewston": Name given to the rich "micro-brewery" scene in the Houston area. Customers can buy beers from some of these breweries at Buc-ee's convenience stores.

"Bricks and mortar": Buc-ee's has very little online presence, doing nearly all of its business in bricks and mortar locations — physical stores. As a result, the company's website is rather basic, listing few details about the many services offered at its many locations. Also, the company does minimal "online" sales for general consumers. Some speculate that Buc-ee's website provides only the most basic information because the company wants to maintain a sense of curiosity about its stores — to lure in the public. However, it's possible that Buc-ee's is simply "sticking to its knitting" by offering a first-rate "bricks and mortar" experience, at the expense of an online presence. Bricks, not clicks.

brisket: The shoulder cut of beef. Generally considered a "tough" portion of meat — unless it is especially prepared. Brisket is often cooked in a very slow cooker to tenderize the meat and to add smoked flavor. Based on the sales volume of its brisket sandwiches, Buc-ee's appears to have this flavorful process "down." "Fresh brisket on the board!"

Brisket biscuit: A scrumptious rhyming treat available at Buc-ee's.

Brisket tacos: A simple, scrumptious food item available at Buc-ee's. Two of your favorite things together: brisket and tacos.

broken fan belt: Time-honored "reason" given by many when asked why they settled in cities such as **Plano, Texas** or **New Braunfels, Texas** while supposedly en route to California, up from San Antonio.

Bronze beaver: Can we keep it "G-rated" please? Buc-ee's larger stores feature a metal statue of the mascot Buc-ee, approximately four feet tall. Another parallel to Disney theme parks, which feature a statue of founder Walt Disney and "mascot" Mickey Mouse.

brotein: Protein-packed snacks, such as "brotein bars", Bueno brand bars, or jerky, are often consumed by bodybuilders and other assorted gym rats. Buc-ee's has a large selection in this category. So, it appears that a strategy is emerging. Head to Buc-ee's and load up on scrumptious snacks. Then head to the gym and "burn off" that brisket.

Bucee-geeking: When someone "geeks out" regarding a visit — especially a first-time visit — to Buc-ee's.

Bucee-licious: Term on Buc-ee's merchandise, which appears to proclaim the store's often scrumptious food offerings. To others, this may appear as a riff on the (R-rated?) term "bootylicious."

Buc-eeneers: Florida nickname for Buc-ee's fans, especially when they are also Tampa Bay Buccaneers fans.

"BUC-EE SAYS RELAX": Slogan on Buc-ee's T-shirts from a few years back, reportedly discontinued and not recently available for sale. A play on the 1980s T-shirts from the band Frankie Goes to Hollywood, whose T-shirts shouted "Frankie Says Relax."

Buc-ee's boogie boards: Buc-ee's sells Buc-ee's branded boogie boards (small surfboards) at Florida locations.

Buc-ee's bucket hats: For sale at many Buc-ee's locations.

"Buc-ee's buggies": Shopping carts that many find a necessity at Buc-ee's. Not often will someone determine that they need a shopping cart at a gas station — except at Buc-ee's and a few other competitors such as Wally's.

Buc-ee's duckies: Yes, Buc-ee's has rubber-duckie bathtub toys available for sale at some locations.

"Buc-ee's List": A mission pursued by some, to visit every Buc-ee's location. A play on the expression "bucket list." As Buc-ee's expands, this gets a bit more challenging — but a bit more tempting, to some — every year.

"(The) Buc-ee's Truck": A vintage pickup truck — or truck replica — circa the 1950s — on display near the center of many of Buc-ee's larger store locations. In most of these trucks, the cargo bed has an abundance of "Buc-ee's" beaver dolls — which of course, are for sale. Some of the trucks are styled as Fords, at least one is a so-called "Studebeaver." Ha-ha. The usually-red "Buc-ee's Trucks" seem to add both to the "retro" feel of Buc-ee's locations, and also to the "destination" or "roadside attraction" appeal.

Example - Husband: *"I've gotta use the restroom."*

Wife: *"Well, I want to check out all the cool souvenirs."*

Husband: *"Meet me at the Buc-ee's Truck in about an hour."*

Wife: *"An hour?"*

"Buc-ee's virgin": Someone who has yet to experience Buc-ee's.

Buffet, Warren: The legendary investor and chief executive officer of Berkshire Hathaway does not have any known affiliation with Buc-ee's. However, it's worth noting that Buc-ee's is the kind of business that Mr. Buffet loves to buy: a well-managed, closely controlled enterprise in a business that is (relatively) easy to understand: gas stations, car washes, and bricks-and-mortar retail. Will Berkshire Hathaway and Buc-ee's ever join forces? Only time will tell.

Burgers: Buc-ee's has all types of sandwiches: sub sandwiches, chicken sandwiches, brisket sandwiches, barbecue sandwiches, and all sorts of creations involving some sort of bread and some sort of meat in the middle — such as kolaches. But Buc-ee's does not feature hamburgers at most of its locations. This is possibly another attempt by Buc-ee's to distinguish themselves from other retailers and from other restaurants. The fact that Buc-ee's does not sell hamburgers at most of its locations... is probably a relief to burger chains — especially Whataburger, which is also based in Texas. **See also... kolaches.**

Burlap bags: Old-school, nostalgia-inducing coarse cloth bags, devised before the age of plastic bags and cellophane wrappers. Buc-ee's sells pecans in burlap bags at many locations. This adds to the nostalgic feel that Buc-ee's seems rather skilled at conjuring.

"Buy four, get two free": Enticing offer related to freshly made fudge squares for sale at Buc-ee's. As if the fudge wasn't fattening enough already. Seems like the slogan should be: "Buy four, get two — two extra pounds on your hips."

buyer's remorse: Discomfort with a recent purchase — or a series of purchases. Faced with a seemingly endless array of snacks, treats, beverages, and souvenirs, customers often bring home "too many" items from Buc-ee's.

Buzzballz: A brand of pre-mixed "cocktails"... in the shape of a ball. Sold in round cans about the size and shape of a billiard ball. "Buzzballz" do have a flat bottom to keep the cans from rolling around — although the flat bottom is hardly visible. For sale at some Buc-ee's locations and at other retailers as well. Quite intoxicating. Or so the author has been told.

"By the pound": At Buc-ee's, you can buy brisket, jerky, and other items "by the pound." At a convenience store. Gas by the gallon, brisket by the pound.

"Byu-sees": Mispronunciation of Buc-ee's sometimes heard on videos on YouTube and elsewhere. Buc-ee's is correctly pronounced "buck-eez."

— C —

Cadillac Desert: Expression relating how the arid American West was remade into a near Garden of Eden. Thanks to dams and canals, vast areas were primed for farming ... and later for sprawling suburbs. The expression *Cadillac Desert* was popularized in the 1986 book of the same name by Marc Reisner.

Example: 1960s-era housing developer # 1: "I'm going to put in a huge housing tract on the edge of Albuquerque."

Developer # 2: "You can't build there. It's desert!"

*Developer # 1: "When I'm done with it, it's gonna be a **Cadillac Desert.**"*

"California carpool": When a group of family members or co-workers drive to the same location — in separate cars.

"Category killer": Description some retail observers use regarding a retailing behemoth which "kills off" several "narrower" retail categories. For instance, it's quite possible that some of Buc-ee's huge "travel center" locations could put out of business —or prevent competitors from opening a business in the first place — in the following categories:

- Bakeries.

- Car washes.

- Gas stations.

- Fast-food restaurants.

- "Ice and water" retailers. (Selling purified water and ice, these retailers are common in the southwestern U.S.)

Circle K: Convenience store chain that is popular in many regions of the U.S., including the western United States. Circle K competes with Buc-ee's in many markets. In recent years, Circle K has improved its fresh food offerings — and especially its coffee selection. Some Circle K locations feature coffee machines that grind the coffee beans a few seconds after the client places his or her order ("pushes the button"): ultra-fresh coffee! Circle K's logo appears to spell out "OK." Circle K now has stores — either company-owned or franchised — throughout North America, Europe, and several Asian countries. Only time will tell if Buc-ee's can match the vast growth of Circle K.

"clunker magnet": Often-reported phenomenon when someone buys a new vehicle. New car owners park their cars at the far end of the parking lot (at Buc-ee's or elsewhere), hoping to avoid dings from other cars that might park nearby. After parking your vehicle at the far end of the parking lot, you go in and buy your barbecue, beer, and other items. When you return to your vehicle, you see a row of four or five vehicles — usually clunkers — surrounding your shiny new car.

"Coffee wall": A "wall" of coffee selections and coffee dispensers available at many Buc-ee's selections. Self-service. One of the many "walls" at Buc-ee's, including the jerky wall and the soda wall. Perhaps fittingly, the "coffee wall" is located just in front of the restrooms.

Colorado: Buc-ee's recently announced plans to open its first

store in the Rocky Mountain State. The company plans to open a store in Johnstown, Colorado, which is about 46 miles north of downtown Denver. It seems to be in keeping with some type of formula...opening "travel centers" about 45 miles from the downtown of the nearest big city.

Convenience Store Woman: Prize-winning, entertaining novel about a young woman living in Japan who doesn't quite fit in — until she gets a job at a convenience store and hums right along with the whirr of the refrigerators and the jingle of the cash registers. This book *just might* resonate with Buc-ee's employees and customers. Written by Sayaka Murata and published in 2016.

Crackseat driver: 1. An erratic, seemingly crack-smoking driver. **2.** A "backseat" driver who gives all sorts of tips and directions to the actual driver, but is the *LAST* person you should take driving instructions from.

"crunchy water": Water in its "solid-state" — ice. Buc-ee's has an amazing quantity of ice freezers on the "outside wall" of its larger locations.

'cue: Texas shorthand for barbecue. Normally contains an asterisk before the "C," as in 'cue.

"Daddy's soda": Term used by toddlers, referring to beer. Buc-ee's has a large selection of "Daddy's soda."

Dallasification: Term used by some in **Austin, Texas,** for growing "over-commercialization" of the city. Both Austin and Dallas have Buc-ee's locations in their respective "extended" greater metro areas... though far from the 1downtowns of either Austin or Dallas.

"Dangerously under caffeinated": World view of many who haven't yet had their first (or second or third) cup of coffee of the day. Buc-ee's happily has many choices in its well-tended-to "Coffee Wall" area — though some coffee snobs may "steer" clear of Buc-ee's.

Daytona Beach: Buc-ee's has a large location near **Daytona Beach, Florida.** Now your two favorite things together: the beach and Buc-ee's! Indeed Buc-ee's is probably an ideal stop on the way to the beach to load up on snacks, drinks, beach floats, sunblock, etc. And ice: Buc-ee's seems to have an endless collection of ice freezers in the front of most of its locations. Some say that Buc-ee's is unlikely to open a location in south Florida because the land for such a massive center would be expensive indeed.

The Daytona Beach Buc-ee's location is a good stop for many headed to South Florida or Walt Disney World.

deadmalls.com: Interesting, somewhat mesmerizing website that tracks the fate of dead or dying shopping malls. Quite intriguing are malls that closed only a few years after opening or that went out of business before they ***even opened*** for business. It's possible that Buc-ee's is partly responsible for this trend of "dying malls," having diverted at least some "mall traffic" — especially regarding food courts and souvenir shops.

"Decision-making process": Thought process or decision-making process of Buc-ee's devotees. The process goes something like this:

"It's for sale at Buc-ee's.."

dessertarian: A sweet tooth: one who emphasizes desserts in their "diet." Buc-ee's is a very tempting retailer for dessertarians, with choices including fresh-made fudge, sweet kolaches, fresh-roasted nuts, and more.

"De*store*nation": A retail "store" such as Buc-ee's which has successfully become a "destination" for shopper, road trippers, and tourists. Hard to beat that.

dimple: A hollow or false bottom on a bottle designed to skimp on contents but maintain the appearance of the same bottle size. Drink vendors at Buc-ee's, and probably at most retailers, have engaged in this practice. **See also: *shrinkflation.***

— E —

Efland, North Carolina: A town in North Carolina in which Buc-ee's had proposed a store location. Efland is about 40 miles northwest of Raleigh. After repeated difficulties in receiving approvals from local officials in North Carolina, Buc-ee's decided not to proceed with plans for opening an Efland location. Buc-ee's officials decided to "F" it, regarding the "Efland" location.

Ennis, Texas: A Buc-ee's location about 35 miles south of Dallas along Interstate 45. In typical Buc-ee's fashion, the location is far from downtown — in this case downtown Dallas. Ennis sounds like ... oops, just remembered this book will be distributed in the Texas State public school system. Or *WAS* gonna be in Texas schools.

Flip flops and tank tops: Semi-official attire at Buc-ee's beach locations.

"Food-induced coma": Haha term for the intense drowsiness which often besets diners after a large or rich meal.

Example: *After visiting Buc-ee's and having a brisket sandwich, sausage on a stick, and Key Lime Pie in a cup, Miguel went into a food-induced coma.*

Fort Worth, Texas: The Buc-ee's location in Fort Worth is an exception to the general rule that Buc-ee's rarely has locations within the city limits of some of the largest cities in Texas.

"Free car washes": Rain. A competitor to the gigantic car washes available at some Buc-ee's locations.

"Freshhh brisket on the board!": Frequent "call and answer" heard when a fresh selection of brisket has been removed from the cooker at Buc-ee's locations. Some get a "rise" from this cheerful expression, some probably tire of this frequent proclamation. "Fressshh Briiii..." Yeah, right. Whatever.

$$- \text{G} -$$

"Gas Pro Shop": Haha nickname for Buc-ee's used by some "YouTubers." In the same vein as the famous outdoor-gear store "Bass Pro Shop," Buc-ee's has a large selection of camping, hunting, and fishing gear. But with a difference: Buc-ee's has endless gas pumps.

"Grand" openings: When Buc-ee's opens a new travel center, it often has the feel of a "Black Friday" event, or the opening of an amusement park. For instance, when the **Daytona Beach, Florida** location opened, customers waited hours in the early morning for the opening. As one politician noted, not often is there a big deal when a gas station opens — except at Buc-ee's.

"Hangover Heaven": Buc-ee's is the ideal stop for those suffering from a hangover. All kinds of coffee, juice, rich foods… or healthful foods… depending which way you "resolve" to go. The only drawback for hangover sufferers is that Buc-ee's has no in-store dining. Although if you're hungover you're probably not so worried about "in-store dining." Or so the author has been told.

"hostile architecture": Term used by some referring to architecture and/or furnishings designed to reduce loitering and — in some cases — make an area unwelcoming to homeless people. An example is bus stops which have individual seats rather than benches, as benches might encourage someone to stretch out and spend the night.

Some also use the term "hostile architecture" to refer to a public area that was designed in part to be — or was later retrofitted to be — unwelcoming to skateboarders.

"(the) Hover technique": Technique used by some when encountering less than trustworthy (dirty) toilet seats at gas stations and elsewhere. Rather than sitting on the toilet, folks will "hover" just above the toilet seat while relieving themselves. This technique requires rather strong, sturdy legs. Thanks to the very clean toilets at their stores, the "hover technique" is not required at Buc-ee's. What a relief! (No pun intended).

Huk: Manufacturer of fishing gear, featured in many Buc-ee's locations. Executives at Huk must have been thrilled when Buc-ee's expanded into Florida in recent years. Many Floridians are avid anglers in both freshwater and saltwater, and fishing is nearly a religion for many in the Sunshine State.

"Ice Cream of the Future": Dippin' Dots brand of ice cream. A supposedly less-fattening form of ice cream, which consists of little spheres or pellets of ice cream, a little bigger than a bee-bee. Available at many Buc-ee's locations. Dippin' Dots ice cream is often sold at amusement parks, sports stadiums, and other "leisure" venues. Finding Dippin' Dots at Buc-ee's is yet another feature which helps elevate Buc-ee's to an "attraction" or "destination" status, rather than "just" the status of a gas station or convenience store. Cool fact: The manufacturer of Dippin Dots ice cream uses ultra-cold liquid nitrogen in the "flash-freeze" process of making this frozen treat.

"ICE": Internal combustion engine. Electric car drivers use this term to refer to gas-powered cars, and "gas-powered" (Ha-ha) drivers. Buc-ee refuels thousands of "ICE" vehicles in a single day at one of its travel centers. However, Buc-ee's has increasingly also been adding electric vehicle chargers at many locations.

"ICE-ing": When someone with a gas-powered car — an "ICE" or internal combustion engine car — parks in the electric-vehicle (EV) charging station space, blocking an electric-car driver from charging their car.

$$-\,J\,-$$

"Jesus boots": Texas slang for sandals. Buc-ee's does sell Jesus boots at its stores — both at Texas locations and at non-Texas locations.

John Daly: An Arnold Palmer (iced tea and lemonade) with vodka added. Named for US golfer John Daly, who enjoyed this drink at clubhouses, and pretty much anywhere else. Most of the ingredients for a rather decent "John Daly" mix are available to Buc-ee's locations — except for the vodka.

— K —

"Keep Austin Weird": Slogan of many in and around **Austin, Texas.** With a few locations on the outskirts of the Austin area, Buc-ee's can claim it has done its part to keep Austin "offbeat" and "fun," but perhaps not quite "weird."

"Keep it between the ditches": Southern/Texas admonition to folks driving home after a drink or two (or three...).

"King of the Chill": A riff on "King of the Hill." A person who has taken relaxing to "new heights." Stopping off at Buc-ee's, and loading up on snacks, drinks, and barbeque/outdoor gear is a pretty decent prerequisite for getting some serious chill on.

Kolaches: Eastern-European fluffy-dough stuffed pastries. These treats can be stuffed with either sweet or savory stuffings. A favorite is a kolache stuffed with "dirty rice" and sausage. Some compare kolaches to the familiar "pig in a blanket" (croissant or other pastry stuffed with sausage). Kolaches were brought to Texas in the 1800s by Czech immigrants, and the treats have been popular in Texas ever since. Many Buc-ee's locations feature a wide selection of freshly-baked kolaches.

Kum & Go: Chain of gas stations/convenience stores primarily in the Midwest and the "Mountain States" region of the U.S. Kum & Go is a competitor regarding Buc-ee's — or will be — as Buc-ee's expands into these regions. Buc-ee's recently announced plans to open a store in Colorado, which is in Kum & Go territory.

— L —

Larger-than-life personalities: A person who is very successful and seems to defy societal and/or normal "business world" conventions. Buc-ee's co-founder Arch Aplin III seems to fit into this mold. Another such personality is Tesla/Twitter/The Boring Company CEO Elon Musk, who recently moved the headquarters of Tesla from the Bay Area of California to the Austin, Texas area. Yet another, who spent most of his years in nearby Arkansas: Sam Walton, founder of Wal-Mart.

"Let's Go Nuts": The catchy sign marking the "nuts" section of Buc-ee's.

— M —

"maphead": Someone who takes great pleasure in maps, geography, travel, and atlases. "Mapheads" most likely will appreciate Buc-ee's "travel centers," a welcome respite for road trippers. This term was popularized by *Jeopardy!* game show champ (and later host) Ken Jennings.

"Maverick": An unconventional person. A rule breaker. Someone who pursues an independent path. Well, Buc-ee's co-founder Arch Aplin probably fits the mold as a "Texas maverick." (Although, if everyone in Texas is a Maverick, then... — well — let's save that for another discussion.)

"meatloaf line": A term used by writer David Brooks of the *New York Times*. Refers to the transition zone where affluent suburbs fade into the countryside. Inside the line, trendy suburbanites rarely eat meatloaf. Outside the line, meatloaf is still a staple. When Buc-ee's builds a new massive "travel center," the stores seem to be located near the "meatloaf line." For instance, the Katy, Texas, location is about 30 miles west of downtown Houston.

Melissa: 1.: Location of a Buc-ee's store in Melissa, Texas. **2.:** A beautiful song by the 1970s band The Allman Brothers, from the Album, *Eat a Peach*.

"Minni-bago": A "mini" or small RV or camper. A riff on the popular "Winnebago" brand of RVs. Many a minni-bago can be seen stopping at Buc-ee's to load up on road-trip supplies. And — to allow the drivers and passengers to use clean, un-cramped restrooms. Though the

"Merchandisers": Industry "insider" term for the ice-freezers or ice boxes which number in the dozens outside of many Buc-ee's locations. As some have noted, Buc-ee's seems to sell ice at 1970s prices.

"mesmerized": The description that some give to their reaction when first walking into a Buc-ee's location... especially the overwhelming selection of snacks and prepared foods.

"Mom-osa": Mimosa cocktail, when consumed by a Mom. A Mimosa contains champagne and chilled citrus juice, usually orange juice. Often consumed at brunch.

NEV: Neighborhood Electric Vehicle. A "golf cart" used to ride around the neighborhood and to run nearby errands. Popular in resort areas of the Sun Belt, where Buc-ee's has many locations.

New Braunfels, Texas: The New Braunfels Buc-ee's location holds the record as the largest convenience store in the world, according to the Buc-ee's website. New Braunfels is a rapidly-growing area and lies between Austin and San Antonio.

Non-Texan: An important distinction. Refers to those who were not born in — or do not live in — the Lone Star State.

"not enough ponies": An underpowered vehicle that does not allow you to overtake someone else's "wagon." An important consideration on road trips.

Nutella: 1. Nickname for a crazy-acting female. **2.** A popular "chocolate and hazelnut" sandwich spread. (The main ingredients of Nutella are actually sugar and palm oil. When the marketing department gets hold of something, **stuff happens**.) Nutella is found in many combinations at convenience stores and other retailers.

— O —

"One of 'em.": Standard — and expected — answer you should give when asked, "Is that your Cadillac?" Or when asked, "Is that your Tesla?"

"Overbite": The signature "overbite" of the Buc-ee's Beaver mascot — whose upper teeth project far over "his" lower teeth. The word "Overbite" is proudly stamped on some Buc-ee's "merch" (merchandise) items and snack items.

— P —

Pecans: Yummy nuts from pecan trees which are quite common in Eastern Texas, where Buc-ee's hails from. In recent decades pecans have become increasingly expensive, yet Buc-ee's somehow still manages to sell pecans in many locations.

"Pecan logs": The hallmark product of a Buc-ee's competitor — Stuck-eys — which also had rest stops for motorists along Interstate highways, especially during the "baby boomer" era. Pecan logs and plenty of other concoctions made with pecans are also available at Buc-ee's. This makes sense seeing as Buc-ee's is Texas-based, and pecan trees are often grown there.

"pet relief area": Buc-ee's prides itself on its well-maintained bathrooms. But the gas station chain has not forgotten about pets! Many Buc-ee's locations feature "pet relief" or "dog walk" areas. Pet owners are encouraged to pick up after their pets.

"Pig in a blanket": Mainstream parallel to kolaches (pronounced koh-lah-cheese). Kolaches are scrumptious baked treats with fillings either sweet or savory. A bit of an oversimplification to simply call kolaches "pig in a blanket," but it does give a reference point about these scrumptious treats. Kolaches originated in the present-day regions of Czech and Hungary in Central Europe. Thankfully, Texas immigrants brought kolaches to Texas in the mid-1800s. These treats are still popular in Texas today.

Pine Curtain: Imaginary dividing line between woodsy East Texas and the much drier West Texas.

"Pit boss": A person in charge of a barbecue pit or generally in charge of food preparation in a barbecue setting. The "pit bosses" at Buc-ee's have quasi "rock star" status.

pizza model: City planning term describing how metro areas often grow in an outward pattern with several new "downtowns" dotting the "pie" surface, resembling a pepperoni pizza. Buc-ee's travel centers can often be found "between the pepperonis" amongst sprawling Texas cities.

"Potty like a rock star": Advertising message on some Buc-ee's billboards.

"Pre-Texans": Folks who haven't moved to Texas *yet,* but will *eventually.*

— Q —

Quail eggs: Buc-ee's features prominently displayed pickled quail eggs available at many of its locations. Another "eye-opener" for many customers. The quail eggs seem to add to the rural appeal that Buc-ee's appears to be "cultivating" at its locations. On the subject of quail eggs, Costco is another notable retailer selling these items. In the winter of 2022-2023, Costco sold fresh quail eggs in the refrigerated area.

It's possible that quail eggs gained popularity during the U.S. chicken egg shortage of late 2022 and early 2023.

"Redneck Riviera": Term referring to the **Florida Panhandle** coast on the Gulf of Mexico. The term "Redneck Riviera" can be used either in a friendly, "haha" way, or in a snooty manner. The **Myrtle Beach, South Carolina** area is sometimes also called "Redneck Riviera." Buc-ee's now has locations near both of these resort areas. Some might suggest that these areas compose a "target demographic" for Buc-ee's.

"Refinery Row": Heavily-industrialized area near **Corpus Christi, Texas.** Buc-ee's got its start not far from this area.

rest areas, state-operated: Buc-ee's could easily be thought of as a private-sector company that provides highway rest areas, which are usually provided by the state highway department or transportation department in most areas. It would be interesting to know if highway departments plan the building — and spacing of their rest stops "around" Buc-ee's locations.

reverse diet: Term for easing your way out of a dietary regimen and gradually returning to a normal food intake. If you want to revert to a "normal" calorie-inducing diet... Buc-ee's is a godsend.

"Roadside attraction": Some Buc-ee's locations appear to continually inch closer to the status of a "roadside attraction" or a "destination" for travelers. Some features associated with a destination or roadside attraction which visitors find at certain Buc-ee's include:

- Car wash conveyor at some locations (including Katy, Texas) which has light show features, in some respects like a low-key amusement ride.

• A heavily featured "mascot"... Buc-ee the beaver.

• An interesting (to most) souvenir selection.

• A penny press, usually found at tourist attractions.

• Foods you often find at amusement parks and tourist attractions, including cotton candy, freshly-made fudge, fresh-roasted nuts, taffy, "Dippin Dots" ice cream and "nostalgia-inducing" candy selections.

"R.V. there yet?": Fun slogan on T-shirts for sale at Buc-ee's locations.

Samples: Buc-ee's does often give samples of items including jerky and fudge. In some cases you need to ask for samples — in some cases the employees proactively offer samples. Seems reasonable — from a business viewpoint — that the company offers samples of jerky, because it is quite expensive. Their jerky isn't janky.

Sausage on a stick: Yes readers, Buc-ee's does sell "sausage on a stick." These are available in the deli area.

scrummy: Food that is scrumptious and yummy. Buc-ee's has many selections that fit into this category, including barbecue, baked goods, and all sorts of snacks.

Sheetz: A regional chain of convenience stores, famous for its "Made To Order" (MTO) submarine sandwiches. As of early 2023, Sheetz had over 600 stores, primarily in Pennsylvania and neighboring states including Maryland, West Virginia, and Ohio. Sheetz also has locations in Virginia and North Carolina. Most of the Sheetz stores also sell gasoline. It appears that Buc-ee's and Sheetz are on a bit of a "collision course" in terms of territory.

Skimpflation: When a retailer provides a lower level of service yet charges the same price or a higher price. This trend has impacted many retailers in the 2020s, including restaurants. Although Buc-ee's has raised prices in the early 20s, it does appear that Buc-ee's has maintained its standards of cheerful service and cleanliness.

"socks and sandals": Favorite footwear of snow birds and others in the Sun Belt area, where Buc-ee's has been expanding rapidly.

"State skipping": Phenomenon in which a rapidly expanding retailer "skips" over a state, or states, in its march of expansion. Buc-ee's did this regarding Louisiana and Mississippi, when expanding from Texas to Alabama. This must sting more than a little for residents of the Texas neighbor-state of Louisiana. Alabama recently got its third Buc-ee's location, and Louisiana has zero locations.

Buc-ee's competitor *Wawa* has also engaged in "state skipping." Wawa has "skipped" over much of the Southeast — expanding from the Mid-Atlantic states to Florida. In the process, Wawa "skipped" over the Carolinas and Georgia, expanding from Virginia to Floridia.

Stories From Texas, Some of Which Are True: Fun book with many (sometimes true) yarns about the Lone Star State. By author W.F. Strong.

stuffed chickens: Another eye opener! Stuffed chickens are available at many Buc-ee's locations, in refrigerated coolers near the jerky section. For instance the Florence, South Carolina Buc-ee's location recently had available whole stuffed chickens. Some of the choices included chickens stuffed with "jalapeno cornbread" or dirty rice. Sounds quite appealing, actually. For someone in their twenties looking for a "bird" to serve at "Friendsgiving," a stuffed chicken might be a convenient option.

Shiner Bock: A Texas-based brand of beer, which Buc-ee's sells in large quantities at many of its locations. Though available in many varieties, a dark lager is one of "Shiner's" favorites. Some — such as "urban explorer", podcaster and YouTuber "WallieB26" — complain that this famous Texas brand of beer is not available at Buc-ee's Florida locations. Shiner Bock is based in **Shiner, Texas.**

Shiner, Texas: City famous as the home of Shiner Bock beer. Shiner is roughly equidistant between Houston and San Antonio. The city is about 120 miles west of downtown Houston.

"Silicon Hills": Term used to describe the **Austin, Texas,** area. Beginning in the 1980s, many tech companies (including Dell) made homes in the "hill country" around Austin. Electric vehicle maker Tesla Inc. recently joined this group by opening a plant (called the "Giga Austin" plant) in the area. In a pattern observed regarding the metro areas of several large Texas cities, Austin does not have any Buc-ee's locations within its "city limits." One of the nearest locations is in Bastrop, Texas, about 30 miles southeast of downtown Austin.

"Silicon Prairie": Name for the **Dallas-Fort Worth** area, due to its many "tech and telecom" companies. Some also refer to the Chicago-Naperville, Illinois, area as the "Silicon Prairie." (Other Midwestern areas also claim this title.) One of the closest Buc-ee's locations to downtown Dallas is in **Terrell, Texas**, about 30 miles east of downtown Dallas.

"SMOG": 1. "Signal. Mirror. Over shoulder. Go!" A safe-driving slogan for beginners (or, umm... others) when changing lanes, backing out of a parking space, or easing out of a gas-pump point. A rather useful term in the often-crowded Buc-ee's parking lots. This term sometimes becomes unwelcome advice when backseat teens eagerly use this phrase on their parents. **2.** A distasteful blend of "smoke and fog." Smog. Considered a Southern California problem — but present in varying degrees in nearly the entire U.S.

"socks and sandals": Semi-official footwear of "snowbirds" when visiting Southern locales, such as south Texas, east Texas, the Gulf coast of the U.S., and Florida. All of these areas have Buc-ee's locations.

Soda selections, Texas-based: Buc-ee's is well known for its massive soda selection. Buc-ee's proudly sells Dr. Pepper and Big Red brands, both of which originated in the **Waco, Texas** area.

Sprouts Farmers Market: Growing grocery chain with an emphasis on cheap yet healthful foods. Sprouts has a large emphasis on produce, including "organic" fruits and vegetables. Prevalent in the western and southeastern U.S., "Sprouts" now has over 50 locations in Texas. A bit of an "anecdote" to Buc-ee's and its emphasis on sweet and salty snacks, and the huge emphasis on soda prevalent at Buc-ee's locations. Sprouts is based in the metro Phoenix, Arizona area.

stalls: Some Buc-ee's locations have 72 stalls in the restroom. Not only are the restrooms generally regarded as very clean, the restrooms are also very large.

steam cleaning: Buc-ee's steam cleans its soda dispenser area and its coffee stations as well. A great selection, in a clean environment.

"struck oil at the altar": Texas slang for marrying into a wealthy family. Nice work if you can get it.

"SUV sandwich": Condition of those driving small cars who inevitably find their cars parked between two oversized, poorly parked sport utility vehicles or pickup trucks.

"Tank tops and flip flops": "Hallmark" or "indicator" items that you're near the beach. Items available at many Buc-ee's locations. Preferably worn together.

Tesla "supercharger" stations: These chargers do exist near the Calhoun, Georgia, location.

Texas City, Texas: Buc-ee's has a popular location in Texas City, Texas on the "Gulf Freeway" between Houston and Galveston. A popular stopping point for those headed to — or from — the beach. Hard to forget what state you're in, when you're in Texas City, Texas.

Texas Monthly: One of the few publications available for purchase at Buc-ee's. *Texas Monthly* journalists often report on the rapid growth of Buc-ee's.

"That is so Texas!": Slang expression, reportedly commonly used in Norway, that means something is "over the top"; crazy. This usage has been reported in *Texas Monthly* and on the website of BBC News. Certainly could apply to some Buc-ee's locations in Texas, reportedly containing the world's largest convenience store, and the world's longest car wash.

"throning": Spending time on the toilet, after one's business, to gain a few moments of quiet time. Sometimes used as a tactic to create a sort of temporary **man cave,** or **she-shed.** Because of Buc-ee's very clean and spacious restrooms, many a parent probably does a little throning in the restrooms to gain a moment of peace and quiet while on a family road trip.

(The) Thumb: Yet another convenience-store/gas station/barbecue joint which *appears* to be emulating the Buc-ee's formula. The Thumb is an upscale convenience store and gas station in swanky north **Scottsdale, Arizona** in the metro Phoenix area. The Thumb is renowned for its fresh barbecue and clean interior and exterior. On its Facebook page, "The Thumb" claims it is a "barbecue/bistro/gas station/car wash/gift shop." Sound familiar? The Thumb was apparently named for a landmark in the nearby McDowell Mountains. "Tom's Thumb" is a very noticeable rocky outcrop or spire which sticks out from the ridgeline of the McDowell Mountains, not far away.

"treasure hunt": Term for a strategy used by retailers such as Costco, Aldi, and Trader Joe's who often wow shoppers with unexpected items. It appears Buc-ee's has adopted this strategy, especially regarding:

- The snack selection, particularly the nostalgic "treat" finds.

- The gift and souvenir selection.

- The outdoor gear items, for fishing, camping, hunting, barbecuing, and picnics. Indeed, the outdoor gear is nearly an attraction in and of itself, causing curious visitors to browse and thereby extend their "rest stop."

"tree nuts": 1. Treats from trees such as cashews, pecans, and pistachios. Buc-ee's features a wide selection of freshly roasted nuts in its "Let's Go Nuts" section near the middle of its "travel center" locations. **2.** "Tree Nuts" refers to folks who employ extreme measures (some say) in defense of trees and in the cause of forest preservation.

truckers: "Eighteen-wheeler" truck rigs are not permitted as customer conveyances at Buc-ee's. Needless to say, some truck drivers (perhaps many) don't appreciate that they are effectively not permitted at Buc-ee's — at least not while driving a big rig. As at least one YouTuber has noted, truckers are "allowed" to bring in essential goods, but are not allowed to "buy" those goods — while driving a big rig.

Turkey jerky: Buc-ee's is well known for its jerky, and the extensive selection includes "turkey jerky." Buc-ee's might not have been the first retailer to use the term "turkey jerky," but was probably ahead of most.

— U —

"U-boat": Retail slang for a large "U"-shaped cart or "dolly" employ-ees use to stock goods on shelves. These long, narrow carts have poles on each end and are open on the sides for easy unloading. The carts do resemble the letter "U" when viewed from the side.

"Vacation goggles": Behavior pattern in which items look more appealing while on vacation. Sometimes leads to "buyer's remorse" after returning home. This can apply to items ranging from souvenirs to "timeshare" enrollments. Yikes! With its many tempting treats, souvenirs, and items of outdoor gear, Buc-ee's is indeed a locale in which "vacation goggles" seem to activate. **See also:** *buyer's remorse.*

Vlog: A video blog (web log), in which a person frequently posts videos about their favorite topics. Visits to Buc-ee's are a frequent topic on many YouTube videos. A vlogger known as "WallieB26" frequently posts videos about his visits to Buc-ee's stores, especially in Texas. As of early 2023, WallieB26 has over 50,000 subscribers.

Volta charging stations: A chain of electric vehicle (EV) charging stations owned by Volta Charging, Inc. In late 2022, Royal Dutch Shell entered an agreement to purchase Volta and its chain of charging stations. As many Buc-ee's customers know, Buc-ee's is increasingly adding EV charging stations to its locations. It appears that competition in the EV "charging industry" is heating up amongst convenience store and gas station chains.

Waco: A city of over 130,000 sitting near the heart of the triangle formed by the cities of Dallas, Houston, and Austin. Waco is along the Brazos River and Interstate 35. The Buc-ee's location near **Temple, Texas** is about 32 miles south of downtown Waco. Buc-ee's recently announced plans for a new location in **Hillsboro, Texas**, about 34 miles *north* of Waco. When the Hillsboro store opens, Waco will be "bracketed" by Buc-ee's stores — both about 30 miles from town.

WallieB26: YouTuber channel which features many video tours of Buc-ee's locations, in both Texas and in southeastern states. The channel often cheerfully focuses on Buc-ee's merchandise such as T-shirts with clever slogans — and on Buc-ee's scrumptious dining options. In addition to tours of Buc-ee's locations, "WallieB" video subjects include touring abandoned retail properties, such as defunct malls, restaurants, and car dealerships. You could say that the channel features retail properties at both ends of their respective lifecycles: new and vibrant — and old and abandoned. Something about this approach makes you appreciate the ordinary — such as a grocery store visit in which the store is open for business and features plenty of employees and customers.

The host — who rarely mentions his "real name" — often ends his videos by cheerfully telling viewers to "stay awesome."

"Walls": The "walls" of merchandise on which Buc-ee's displays merchandise, especially food items. When Buc-ee's says they have a "Wall of Jerky," they mean it. Buc-ee's has dozens of varieties of jerky hanging from hooks on the "wall." Other "walls" include:

- Coffee wall.

- Soda wall.

- "Old Faves" wall (nostalgic candy and snack selections).

- Ice walls. Rows of freezers (called "merchandisers") filled with bags of ice.

- Nut wall. (Something about the phrase "Nut Wall" sounds a bit sketchy.)

Wally's: A convenience store or "travel center" chain in the Midwest. Wally's as of early 2023 has two stores which are open, plus one under construction. Wally's calls itself "Home of the Great American Road Trip." Wally's seems to follow the "Buc-ee's formula" in many respects. For instance, Wally's claims to have:

- An abundance of gas pumps.

- A spacious interior with an emphasis on freshly-prepared food.

- Clean restrooms.

Wawa: This Philadelphia-area based convenience store chain is a competitor regarding Buc-ee's in many respects. Wawa's fresh food selection is a hit with customers, many of whom are multi-generational Wawa consumers. Custom-order freshly-made sandwiches are a favorite at Wawa. Though most of its locations are in and around the "mid-Atlantic" states of Pennsylvania, Delaware, Maryland, and Virginia, Wawa now has locations in Florida.

Thus Florida has become a bit of a battleground state — two convenience store chains with cult (or near-cult) followings have expanded from their home states and now compete in Florida. Buc-ee's now has two large "travel center" locations in Florida: Daytona Beach and St. Augustine, in competition with Wawa. This aspect adds to the fun of Florida road trips — allowing more selection for customers and allowing your "inner food critic" to compare Buc-ee's and Wawa.

"Weaponized": Haha term for extremely spicy foods, such as the many varieties of jerky — and the many sauces found — at Buc-ee's.

Example: Wife: *"I think I'm going to try that Cajun-style jerky at Buc-ee's."*

Husband: *"Okay but, I warned you. It's been weaponized."*

West Texas: A sprawling region of the state of Texas — and indeed of the nation as a whole. This region only recently got its first Buc-ee's location. In December, 2024 Buc-ee's opened its first West Texas location in Amarillo. For many years the dearth of locations in West Texas was a cause for concern (dare we say "whining?") amongst West Texans.

"What all the 'fuss' is about": Refrain often heard when someone (especially a non-Texan) visits a Buc-ee's for the first time. The key reasons given for "the fuss" — or perhaps even a cult following — are:

- Very tasty barbecue and other "yummy" freshly prepared foods.

- Ultra-clean restrooms.

- The fun but cheesy "roadside attraction" billboard slogans.

• A nearly endless selection of sodas, coffee flavors, and other refreshments.

• A fun souvenir area, reminiscent of "Route 66"-style gift shops.

• Dare we say the "charming" Buc-ee's beaver mascot, found on just about anything at Buc-ee's.

Example: Wife: *"Why are you stopping at that 'Byoosees' place'? We just got gas a little while ago."*

Husband: *"I wanna see what all the fuss is about — at Buc-ee's."*

"Whatastore": An example of a "fellow" Texas-based retailer which does have a robust online store selling all sorts of merchandise. Whataburger sells its branded t-shirts, hats, and other items on its "Whatastore" app and website. Some say that Buc-ee's is missing out on an opportunity to monetize or "cash in" on its appeal by not having a bigger "web commerce" presence. Although shoppers can buy quite a few Buc-ee's items via Amazon, Buc-ee's had little web sales via its own websites as of early 2023.

"When in Rome": Buc-ee's recently opened its first location in north Georgia (the state in America, not the country near Russia). This location is near Rome, Georgia. Next up: A location (perhaps) in Rome, Italy?

Example: *"When in Rome, visit Buc-ee's."*

wine o'clock: Happy hour. Vino drinking time, which varies from participant to participant. But generally, the sooner the better. Buc-ee's has a rather decent vino selection in many of its store.

Wisconsin: Buc-ee's in early 2023 announced plans to launch its first store in the Midwest. The San Antonio News-Express reported that Buc-ee's has begun plans for a store in **DeForest, Wisconsin.** DeForest is about 15 miles north of Madison, Wisconsin and is about 80 miles west of Milwaukee. This will be Buc-ee's first store outside of the "greater South" — if you include Texas and Kentucky as part of the "South."

World's largest convenience store: According to the Buc-ee's website, the **Sevierville, Tennessee** location had this honor as of mid 2023.

World's longest car wash: Buc'ee's claims that its **Katy, Texas** location had this honor as of early 2023. The car wash in the Katy location is also notable for having a "light show" aspect to a certain extent. Katy is about 30 miles west of downtown Houston. In fact, Katy is nearly due west of Houston — along Interstate 10 — which runs west from Houston.

"Worsh shed": "Worsh shed" is fun southern slang for "wash shed." Therefore, the Katy, Texas Buc-ee's car wash is the world's longest "worsh shed."

(Gen) XXL: Term for overweight members of Generation Z (Gen Z; born mid-1990s to mid-2000s), named for the XXL symbol for *double extra-large* on clothing tags. Perhaps a beacon — or warning — to those who frequent the "soda wall," or the "old faves" candy section, or the fudge counter, or — you get the idea — at Buc-ee's.

"XXL Brisket": Extra-extra large brisket sandwich available at some Buc-ee's locations in March of 2023. Careful so as to avoid the need for "XXL" clothing.

"YIMBY": "Yes in my backyard." Pro-development movement that has sprung up in recent years, as a response to the **NIMBY (Not In My Back Yard)** movement. YIMBIES are often active in cities where housing has become prohibitively expensive. YIMBIES also often favor large-scale housing projects, to the disdain of single-family home proponents. YIMBIES and NIMBIES both get involved in some areas when a retailer announces plans for a large retail location in the area.

Buc-ee's usually receives a "yes in our backyard" response from officials — and perhaps also from the local residents generally — when beginning the permitting process for a new location. One notable exception was Efland, North Carolina. In the early 2020s Efland officials opposed a Buc-ee's location in the area. As of early 2023, Buc-ee's has not announced any plans to renew its efforts to open a store in the area.

Some folks oppose "big-box" retailers generally. In the case of Buc-ee's, it's a bit more difficult to discern whether the company is a "big box" retailer. At first glance, the company's locations may appear as more of a "mid-box" retailer when compared to giant Walmart "supercenters."

"You poor son of a bitch": Expression saying "It sucks to be you."

Example:

Co-worker # 1: "So did you stop at Buc-ee's during your trip to Texas?"

Co-worker # 2: "Well, my wife has been on a health kick lately, cooking all sorts of tofu-based dishes, and she said we shouldn't stop at Buc-ee's."

Co-worker # 1: "You poor son of a bitch."

$$-\,Z\,-$$

"zap map": Slang for an app which helps drivers of electric cars find charging stations. Some Buc-ee's locations, such as the **Florence, South Carolina** store, do feature chargers for electric cars — in addition to countless gas pumps. When capitalized, "Zap Map" is the name of a company and an app in the United Kingdom which assists drivers of electric cars in planning route maps and charging stops.

"Zoom-burb": A very rapidly growing suburb. During the COVID pandemic, many suburbs experienced growth when office workers no longer had to commute (some say "schlep") to downtown office buildings. According to a study by Rice University, the suburbs of Austin experienced much of this growth. From a Buc-ee's perspective, this meant that "Travel Center" stores which were once fairly distant from cities began to appear surrounded by far-flung suburbs.

— Dictionary, continued —

Numbers:

64: Number of selections available at the soda fountain — often called a "soda wall" — at some of Buc-ee's larger locations.

120: Some of Buc-ee's larger travel centers have 120 gas pumps or "fueling positions."

$999.00: Price of a prefabricated "deer stand" (a shelter and hunting blind for hunting deer). The author recently saw a model on display at the Katy, Texas Buc-ee's location in 2022. The cylindrical shelters (looking a bit like a flattened seven-feet high dome — or a gigantic salt shaker) might make a half-decent shed in someone's backyard.

54,000: Square footage of many Buc-ee's "Travel centers." That's about the size of five or six small- to medium-sized convenience stores! At least a few locations are larger.

This marks the end of the Buc-ee's Dictionary — but not the end of our look at the Buc-ee's "cult" phenomenon. We will continue our look at Buc-ee's in the next chapter by looking at the many Buc-ee's locations — and at nearby attractions.

Chapter Five

— Buc-ee's Locations —

Orientation:

In this section, we have listed Buc-ee's locations alphabetically first by state, and then secondarily by municipality within each state. The locations within each state are also listed alphabetically. Needless to say, this means that this section will begin with Alabama, and will end with... Texas, for the moment. In early 2023, Buc-ee's announced plans for a location in Wisconsin, not far from Madison. Planning and construction of stores often takes around 1.5 years, but can often take longer, depending on permitting, etc. A period of about 1.5 years is probably a reasonable amount of time, noting the large size of many Buc-ee's locations.

For many of the locations, we'll spice up the discussion by mentioning nearby attractions and geographical quirks of the area.

Geographic Span of Buc-ee's Locations:

Thought of as a "mostly-Texas" phenomenon, Buc-ee's locations now stretch from south-central Texas to eastern South Carolina. A distance of nearly 1,260 miles, if measured from the New Braunfels, Texas location to the Florence, South Carolina location. Buc-ee's also has locations in Alabama, Florida, Georgia, Kentucky, and Tennessee.

— ALABAMA —

First, a few notes about Buc-ee's rather aggressive expansion into Alabama in recent years. Alabama was the first state outside Texas in which Buc-ee's opened a store. As of early 2023, Buc-ee's has four locations open in Alabama — more locations than any state except Texas. The Alabama locations nearly appear to be "stacked" in a rough north-to-south orientation in this state. There is hardly a spot in Alabama that is more than a 90 minute drive from a Buc-ee's location. Few if any other states can claim this. Well then, what about Texas? East and central Texas have myriad Buc-ee's locations. But West Texas and South Texas have few locations as of early 2023. One could also make a fairly decent case that north Texas also has "less than its share" of Buc-ee's locations. Here are the Alabama locations:

Athens, Alabama:

The Athens location opened in 2023 along Interstate 65 and it's about 23 miles west of downtown **Huntsville,** in northern Alabama. This store is about 10 miles north of the Tennessee River. (Yes, the Tennessee River — ignoring its name — meanders into northern Alabama.)

A fun observation regarding Buc-ee's locations in the southeastern U.S.: several of these stores are in cities — or are near cities — named after famous and ancient European cities. Examples include the **Athens, Alabama** and **Florence, South Carolina** stores. In addition, the **Calhoun, Georgia** location is only about 20 miles from **Rome, Georgia.**

Auburn, Alabama:

This store opened in April, 2023. It's along Interstate 85 about 50 miles northeast of **Montgomery, Alabama.** The Auburn store is just a few miles southwest of Auburn University and is an ideal stop for those heading to and from Auburn Tigers football games. Other nearby cities include **Opelika**, about 7 miles northeast of the Auburn Buc-ee's store.

Example: Co-worker #1: *"What are you gonna do on your trip to Alabama?"*

Co-worker #2: *"I'm going to check out Auburn and Opelika."*

Co-worker #1: *"Opelika. Hope you like it."*

Leeds, Alabama:

The Leeds location is along Interstate 20, about 20 miles east of downtown **Birmingham, Alabama.** The Leeds location is 30 miles west of the semi-legendary Talladega Superspeedway ("Dega") motor sports complex. The Leeds, Alabama Buc-ee's store makes a great "pit stop" for "pit crews" traveling to and from "Dega."

Loxley, Alabama:

If you had to pick one Buc-ee's location to visit this store would probably be one of the most fun. This location is along interstate 10, not far from **Mobile, Alabama** and only about a 50 minute drive from the beaches of **Gulf Shores, Alabama.** This location is also only about 35 miles northwest of **Pensacola, Florida.** The Loxley store is also only about 20 miles west of the Alabama-Florida "state line," in this part of the country formed by the Perdido River. (Perdido means "lost" in Spanish.)

The Loxley location is sometimes referred to as the **"Robertsdale"** location. The store is next to the intersection of I-10 and the Baldwin Beach Express highway, about 30 miles north of Gulf Shores. Not far from this store are the many sights and sounds of Mobile Bay, including the USS Alabama — a World War II-era battleship and interpretive center. Exciting just thinking about it: Buc-ee's... and the beach.

Tesla has installed a "bank" or row of Tesla Supercharging stations next to the Loxley location. This appears to be a growing trend: charging companies and Electric Vehicle (EV) makers installing charging stations at or nearby Buc-ee's locations.

That's it for the Alabama Buc-ee's locations. Four locations in a not-particularly large state. A very decent showing. Can you guess which state is next? A reminder that this guide to Buc-ee's locations is in alphabetical order by state as of early 2024. Read on for the answer.

Florida is one of the largest states east of the Mississippi — a huge market. As of mid-2023 there's only two Buc-ee's locations in the Sunshine State. Both stores are in Florida "East Coast" cities: Daytona Beach and St. Augustine. As of mid-2023, Buc-ee's has no locations in South Florida or in the "Florida Panhandle." But, the Loxley, Alabama location is only about 20 miles west of the western edge of the Florida Panhandle.

The Sunshine State has become a very competitive market for convenience store chains with "cult followings." Two such chains have expanded from their home states and now compete in Florida. Philadelphia-based Wawa, Inc. now has many stores in Florida. Wawa's deli and freshly-made sandwiches are a hit with customers. And Buc-ee's now has two massive "travel center" stores in Florida: Daytona Beach and St. Augustine, in competition with Wawa.

Daytona Beach:

The Daytona Beach location is along Interstate 95 which skirts the east coast of Florida, at the intersection of LPGA Boulevard.

The Daytona location is only about eight miles from nearby beaches — probably closer than most other Buc-ee's locations regarding beaches. The entire Daytona Beach area could be viewed as a celebration of "car culture." Some examples:

> • The Daytona International Speedway, home of the famous annual Daytona 500 NASCAR motor race.

> • Driving and parking on the beach is permitted at Daytona Beach. As of early 2023, a permit is required to drive or park on the beach. Permits are typically $20 and are good for one day during daylight hours.

> • And now: Buc-ee's. The "Travel Center" — near the beach and the speedway — with over 100 gas pumps and endless snacks and drinks. A road tripper's dream.

The Daytona Beach location is near Florida's "Fun Coast." Walt Disney World Resort is about 83 miles to the southwest, on the south side of **Orlando.**

Other interesting notes regarding the Daytona Beach location:

> • Tesla has installed "Superchargers" in a parking lot next door. Juice up your EV while perusing the tempting snacks in Buc-ee's. Not bad at all.

- The Daytona Beach location is about 60 miles north of the **St. Augustine, Florida** Buc-ee's location. A pattern many will notice — in areas with a concentration of Buc-ee's massive "Travel Centers," the locations are about 60 to 90 miles apart.

Ocala (planned location): Buc-ee's in early May, 2023 announced plans to open a store in Ocala, Florida, along Interstate 75.

The location will be near a planned interchange of NW 49th Street and I-75, just north of Ocala. The Ocala location will be about 80 miles northwest of downtown Orlando, Florida.

St. Augustine:

The St. Augustine Buc-ee's location is along Interstate 95, near I-95's intersection with International Golf Parkway. The Parkway is named for the following nearby attractions:

- World Golf Village (a massive golf-themed housing and retail area).

- The World Golf Hall of Fame.

The St. Augustine store is about 13 miles or a 25 minute drive from the famous old Spanish fort and the grounds of the Castillo de San Marcos National Monument. This location, in the region known as Florida's "First Coast," also has adjacent Tesla superchargers. Only about 2.5 miles southwest of the St. Augustine Buc-ee's, travelers can find a Publix supermarket. Publix is a Florida-based chain with a very devoted following.

The nearest beaches are about 20 miles east of the St. Augustine Buc-ee's location. Allow about 35 minutes for driving.

The St. Augustine store is about 30 miles south of downtown **Jacksonville, Florida**. The store is about 60 miles south of the "Georgia-Florida" state line. In this part of the country, "state line" is formed by winding, twisting St. Mary's River, which helps drain the nearby Okefenokee Swamp.

Regarding other Buc-ee's locations, the St. Augustine location is 407 miles — or over a five-hour drive east — of the Loxley, Alabama location which is near Mobile. The St. Augustine location is about 277 miles — or about a four hour drive — southeast of the **Warner Robins, Georgia** location.

— GEORGIA —

The "Peach State" is a rather large state for an East Coast state. In fact, Georgia is the largest state east of the Mississippi. A lot of ground for Buc-ee's to cover. As of May of 2023, Buc-ee's has only two locations in Georgia, both along Interstate 75 which cuts a path through western Georgia on its way to Florida.

Adairsville, Georgia:

The Adairsville location is along Interstate 75 in northwestern Georgia, about a one-hour drive north of Atlanta. Driving south, the next Buc-ee's location is about 180 miles, or roughly a three-hour drive south in Warner Robins, Georgia. The Adairsville location is sometimes referred to as the Calhoun location.

Fun note for electric car users. Tesla has a "supercharger" station adjacent to the Adairsville Buc-ee's location. This is a rather happy combination. A rest stop with excellent food and clean bathrooms near a Tesla "supercharging" location.

Warner Robins, Georgia:

The location is along Interstate 75, about 97 miles or a 1.5 hour drive south of Atlanta. The Warner Robins location is near the exit for Russell Parkway. Though near Warner Robins, the location has a Fort Valley, Georgia address.

This location will be a popular stop for Atlantans heading to Florida on vacation. As Buc-ee's continues its expansion in the region, these vacationers will be able to take care of most of their fueling, snack, and bathroom needs. Buc-ee's in May of 2023 announced plans to break ground for a new location in **Ocala, Florida.** When opened the Ocala location will also be along I-75. The Ocala location will be about 280 miles south of the Warner Robins, Georgia location.

The Warner Robins location is about 15 miles west of Robins Air Force Base. The Warner Robins Buc-ee's location does have adjacent Tesla Superchargers.

Richmond, Kentucky:

"Kentucky Buc-ee's." Buc-ee's recently opened its first store in the Bluegrass State in **Richmond, Kentucky.** The store is along Interstate 75 and is about 30 miles south of **Lexington, Kentucky.** If Lexington is not a sufficient landmark for you, we will add that the Richmond, Kentucky location is about 110 miles south of **Cincinnati, Ohio.** Considering that Buc-ee's was a Texas-only phenomenon as recently as 2019, the chain is displaying a rather decent build-out along Interstate 75, which runs from the Canadian border to south Florida.

For those readers who have been asking, the Richmond Buc-ee's location is about a 1.5 hour drive southeast of the Evan Williams distillery in Louisville, Kentucky. In fact, several locations in the "Bourbon Trail" of distilleries dot nearby Kentucky. The Evan Williams distillery offers tours and samples, though ticket purchases are often required.

I-75 crosses the Kentucky River about 25 miles north of the Richmond location. In fact, the meandering Kentucky River lies on three sides of Richmond, Kentucky: to the east, north, and west.

As of mid-2023, the Richmond, Kentucky location is one of Buc-ee's northernmost locations.

Some travelers, perhaps unfairly, put South Carolina in either of two categories:

1. A place with lots of beaches and the fun port city of Charleston.
2. A region you pass through on the way to Florida.

Well, travelers can add a new attraction: Buc-ee's. The chain opened its Florence, South Carolina location in May of 2022. In the summer of 2023, Buc-ee's began work on a second location in western South Carolina, near Anderson.

Anderson, South Carolina (planned):

Buc-ee's announced in 2022 that the company plans to build a new store near the northwestern "corner" of the quasi-diamond shaped state of South Carolina. The location will be along the intersection of Interstate 85 and Liberty Highway, about 15 miles southeast of college football powerhouse Clemson University. Some facts about the planned Anderson location:

- The location will open in 2025, according to Buc-ee's.

- Land clearing for the site began in 2023.

- The proposed Anderson location is along Interstate 85, which runs through the heart of The Piedmont region of north Georgia and the Carolinas.

• The Anderson location will be about 120 miles northeast of downtown Atlanta, Georgia. But the Anderson store won't be particularly far from suburbs which sprawl northeast of Atlanta. For instance, the Anderson location is 96 miles from Duluth, Georgia.

Attractions and cities around the Anderson location include:

• The gigantic Lake Hartwell. One "arm" of this lake is less than a mile from the planned Buc-ee's store location. Lake Hartwell was formed primarily by damming the Savannah River, although some valleys of tributary rivers were also flooded and added to the size of the lake.

• Greenville, South Carolina. The city is about 20 miles northeast of the planned Anderson store. A Greenville attraction is "Falls Park on the Reedy," a remarkably striking park with waterfalls and pedestrian-friendly bridges in the heart of downtown.

Florence, South Carolina:

The Buc-ee's store in Florence, SC, is along Interstate 95 and is near the I-95 exit used by many when driving to Myrtle Beach — a popular destination. The Florence store is about 67 miles from the nearest beaches in Myrtle Beach. South Carolina is a "diamond" shaped state, indeed shaped like a cut diamond. The Buc-ee's location in Florence then is near the right-hand (or "northeast") point of the diamond shape — called the "girdle" in jeweler's lingo).

The Florence location does feature quite a few charging stations for electric vehicles. Tesla recently announced plans to allow owners of "non-Tesla" vehicles to charge at some of its charging stations. However, Tesla has not announced the exact time frames for this "roll out" to "non-Tesla" owners.

Yet another so-called "border state" which Buc-ee's has entered, along with Kentucky. When an ultra-Texas company expands into Tennessee, it seems like there has to be some story behind this trend. For instance, this reminds you of country crooner George Strait's *All My Ex's Live in Texas*. (Interestingly, the George Strait song mentions several Texas cities which have Buc-ee's locations in the respective cities or nearby.)

Crossville, Tennessee:

Fittingly named, as the location is an ideal stop for those crossing the state of Tennessee or more broadly the Tennessee-Kentucky region.

The Crossville location is along Interstate 40 near the intersection of Genesis Road. The location is about 120 miles or about a two-hour drive east of downtown Nashville, Tennessee. It's about 69 miles or a one-hour drive west of Knoxville. Both of these cities are also along I-40.

The Crossville location does feature adjacent Tesla superchargers: this appears to be the case for nearly all of the locations Buc-ee's has opened outside of Texas in the last few years. Increasingly, many Texas locations also have Tesla superchargers — or superchargers are located nearby.

Some points of interest within two miles or less of the Crossville Buc-ee's location include:

- Stonehaus Winery.

- Flying Pig BBQ.

● An RV park known as "Paradise on the Mountain RV Park." Visitors will notice a pattern that many Buc-ee's travel centers seem to be located near RV dealerships and RV parks.

Not far away is the Obed River, apparently named for a character in the Old Testament. And upstream quite a few miles on the Obed River is the Ohmigod Rapids! Quite an amusing name. A "pre-OMG" name for the rapids.

Sevierville, Tennessee:

As of mid-2023, this "Gateway to the Smoky Mountains" location is the largest Buc-ee's location — and the largest gas station by Buc-ee's or any other retailer — in the world, Buc-ee's claims.

The Sevierville location:

● Opened in June of 2023, and has 128 "fueling positions" (gas pumps).

● Is along Interstate 40, about 20 miles east of Knoxville, Tennessee.

● Is about 25 miles north of the Great Smoky Mountains National Park.

● Is about 90 miles northwest of the popular vacation city of Asheville, North Carolina. Because of its high elevation — and because of its trendiness — Asheville is sometimes called "The Coolest Place in the South."

• The Sevierville store features on its grocery shelves the ever-popular Bush's Beans brand of canned beans. These beans are flavored with bacon, spices, sugar, and molasses. The store is also near the "hometown" of Bush's Beans, a welcome picnic and cookout side dish. Items such as Bush's Beans are in keeping with Buc-ee's down-home, outdoorsy emphasis. The headquarters for Bush Brothers and Company is in nearby Knoxville, Tennessee.

• The Sevierville store is home to a total of 24 on-site Tesla Superchargers, which are electric vehicle charging stations for Teslas — and for many other vehicle brands beginning in 2024. Dare we say Tesla and Buc-ee's are making the Smoky Mountains a little less "smoky"?

• The Sevierville store is the second location in Tennessee. The first location is in Crossville, about 90 miles west of the new Sevierville location. Both locations are along Interstate 40. Therefore, the city of Knoxville, Tennessee, is nearly "bracketed by Buc-ee's." A classic Buc-ee's location strategy... with stores about 40 or 50 miles on either side of a metropolitan area.

• Is located near the city of Sevierville, pronounced "*severe*-ville" by many, though not necessarily by all. The location is sometimes listed as **"Kodak, Tennessee."** Kodak is a community that lies partly within the city limits of Sevierville and partly just north of Sevierville. An 1890s-era postmaster named the community of Kodak. He wanted — and found — an easy-to-spell, easy-to-remember name for the community now called Kodak.

• Sevierville is about 896 feet above sea level, leading to relatively mild summers — compared to much of the South.

• Is an ideal "stop off" for those engaging in camping "and such" in the Great Smoky Mountains, thanks to the large selection of outdoor gear at Buc-ee's.

Points of interest near the Sevierville Buc-ee's location include:

• The French Broad River, which is the butt of many "Dad jokes."

• Mystic Mountain Witch Tours. This tourist attraction is about 40 miles east of the Sevierville Buc-ee's, in the Liberty Hill, Tennessee, area.

• Dumplin Creek, Dumplin Valley Road, and "Dumplin Creek Critter Care" (a pet boarding business, or "dog sitter"). All are near the Buc-ee's location in Sevierville. An annual event in the area is the "Dumplin Valley Bluegrass Festival."

• A distillery known as "Shine Girl." Shine Girl is about 10 miles south of the Sevierville Buc-ee's store.

• An amusement park known as "Goats on the Roof of the Smoky Mountains." A key attraction: the "Goat Coaster," sometimes described as an "alpine roller coaster." Other features of the amusement park include "gem mining." Goats on the Roof of the Smoky Mountains amusement park is near Pigeon Forge, Tennessee, about 18 miles south of the Sevierville Buc-ee's location.

● Forbidden Caverns. This "tourist cave" is about 25 miles southeast of Sevierville and features an underground river and an underground lake. With All of these subterranean bodies of water, maybe the attraction should also include a submarine.

● Dollywood, a theme park owned partly by country music singing legend Dolly Parton. The park features thrill rides and the arts, crafts, and traditional music of the Great Smoky Mountains area. Dollywood is in Pigeon Forge, Tennessee and is about 30 miles southeast of Knoxville, and is about 15 miles south of the Sevierville Buc-ee's location. Dolly Parton was born in Sevierville.

● It appears there's a wide variety of attractions in the Sevierville area.

"Two-Store" States:

With the opening of the Sevierville store, Tennessee has joined the ranks of states with at least two Buc-ee's locations. Other states in this "elite" group include Texas, of course, along with Alabama, Florida, and Georgia. This could be considered a "stack" of states, beginning with Florida, then the "book-end" states of Alabama and Georgia in the second level... and Tennessee as the crown. (Kentucky is the northernmost state with a Buc-ee's store in this region. However, Kentucky only has one Buc-ee's location as of mid-2023.)

That's it for Tennessee locations. Can you guess what state is next?

— TEXAS —

Yes folks, the "star" of the show has arrived — the Lone Star state of Texas. Largest of the "Lower 48" contiguous U.S. states. A lot of ground for Buc-ee's to cover, and plenty of Buc-ee's locations there. As of the writing of this book, Texas is the only state with the smaller "neighborhood"-style Buc-ee's locations. Many of these smaller locations are in the Lake Jackson and Angleton area... where Buc-ee's originated. This area begins about 40 miles south of central Houston.

Readers will note that Buc-ee's locations nearly "surround" these metro areas:

- Dallas-Fort Worth

- Houston.

To a lesser extent, the Austin area is nearly surrounded, though the stores are quite a distance from downtown Austin. Austin-area stores are in some cases forty to sixty miles from downtown Austin.

TEXAS LOCATIONS:

Alvin, Texas:

The location is along Highway 35 North Bypass. The location is about 32 miles south of downtown Houston.

Angleton, Texas (three locations):

Buc-ee's has three locations in Angleton, Texas. Angleton is about 51 miles south of central Houston. The locations here are mostly smaller neighborhood locations, not the gigantic "travel centers." However, the smaller locations are still quite popular with customers.

That's it for locations under the letter "A." At the moment, no Abilene location — *YET!*

Bastrop, Texas:

A large Buc-ee's location. Tesla has installed high-speed electric-vehicle "superchargers" in an adjacent strip of land. The Bastrop location is about 37 miles east-southeast of downtown Austin, Texas. The Bastrop location is about 40 miles north of the interestingly-named city of *Flatonia, Texas.*

Baytown, Texas:

The Buc-ee's store address in Baytown is 4080 East Freeway. The location is about 20 miles east of central Houston. The Baytown store is along Interstate 10, on the way to Louisiana. This location is in the "Refinery Row" area which features many oil refineries and related industries. Probably no one would be surprised if someone one day announced that Buc-ee's has at least considered running a gasoline pipeline from nearby oil refineries to some of its Houston-area locations.

Brazoria, Texas:

The city of Brazoria is named for the Brazos River.

The Brazoria Buc-ee's store is about eight miles west of Lake Jackson, Texas, and is about 50 miles south of central Houston.

Cypress Texas:

This location is in the northwestern portion of metro Houston, Texas — helping form the pattern of Buc-ee's around greater Houston. The location is along highway U.S. 290.

Denton, Texas:

The Denton location is along Interstate 35-E, about 35 miles northwest of downtown Dallas and about 25 miles north of DFW International Airport — perhaps within reach for a quick visit next time you fly to Dallas-Fort Worth. Dallas... and Denton.

The location does feature adjacent Tesla "supercharger" charging stations. Tesla added eight charging stations in land adjacent to the Denton Buc-ee's in May of 2023.

Big news for electric vehicle users — Tesla opened up most of its charging stations to Ford electric vehicles in the year 2024.

Eagle Lake, Texas: The location is in downtown Eagle Lake on Main Street. The store is near the edge of Buc-ee's original or "homeland territory" which features smaller, neighborhood Buc-ee's locations. The Eagle Lake store is about 75 miles northwest of Lake Jackson, Texas (Buc-ee's "birthplace"); and the location is about 60 miles west of downtown Houston, Texas.

Eagle Lake is in rice-growing country. Nearby towns with interesting names include: Nada, Bonus, and Egypt.

Ennis, Texas:

Along Interstate 45. About 30 miles south-southeast of downtown Dallas, Texas. Part of the "ring" of Buc-ee's locations nearly surrounding the Dallas-Fort Worth area.

The Ennis location features nearby Tesla supercharger stations.

Fort Worth, Texas:

The Fort Worth store is about 22 miles north of downtown Fort Worth, and is about 19 miles north of the landmark Fort Worth Stockyards.

One of the few Buc-ee's locations in a somewhat "big-name" city — Fort Worth — and probably the only *Texas location* in a "big-name" city, as opposed to small cities which lie well spaced between major metro centers. For instance the Buc-ee's location-cities of "Luling, Texas," and "Robertsdale, Alabama" are not exactly household names.

(Outside of Texas, Buc-ee's does have two locations in easily recognizable cities: Daytona Beach, Florida; and St. Augustine, Florida.)

The Fort Worth store has an address of 15901 N Freeway, and is along Interstate 35W north of downtown Fort Worth. The location is just a few miles from Texas Motor Speedway. Another pattern of Buc-ee's locations — many of the stores appear to be located near major speedways or "motor sports" venues.

Some "fun spots" for the family near the Fort Worth location include: Ninja Kidz Trampoline Park, about eight miles from Buc-ee's. Ninja Kidz is along Tarrant Parkway.

Freeport, Texas. Two Buc-ee's locations:

The two Freeport stores have these addresses:

- 4231 E. Highway 332.

- 1002 N Brazosport Boulevard.

Buc-ee's has two of its smaller neighborhood locations in Freeport, Texas, which is about 50 miles south of downtown Houston. The Freeport locations are only about eight to twelve miles from Surfside Beach on the Gulf of Mexico. For another point of orientation, the two Freeport stores are about 40 miles southwest of Galveston, Texas. Freeport is also near the mouth of the Brazos River, as the river discharges into the Gulf of Mexico.

Freeport is in "bayou" country. Just a few blocks from the Highway 332 Buc-ee's store is East Union Bayou. Not surprisingly, seafood restaurants are easy to find near the Freeport locations.

Giddings, Texas:

The location is along Highway U.S. 290 and is about 55 miles east of Austin, Texas. The Giddings location is a bit of a rarity: a smaller neighborhood location which is quite a distance (over 100 miles) from the metro Houston area. The Giddings store is part of a string of Buc-ee's locations along Highway 290 stretching west from metro Houston. Other locations include Cypress and Waller. The Cypress store is about 25 miles northwest of downtown Houston; the Waller store is about 52 miles northwest of central Houston.

Example: Texas Mom #1: *"Why are you so giddy?"*

Texas Mom #2: *"Because I'm going to the Buc-ee's... in Giddings."*

Katy, Texas:

This location is one of Buc-ee's massive travel centers. The store is about 30 miles due west of downtown Houston along Interstate 10. The Katy location features what Buc-ee's claims is the world's longest car wash, and it is quite massive.

When the author visited the Katy location in 2022, the store seemed clean and well organized. For instance, all of the soda fountains and coffee stations were quite clean and fully functional. Even the rather large parking lot areas and gas pump areas were quite clean and nearly free of litter. But even better, the employees were cheerful and friendly.

The Katy store is in an important rice-growing region. Katy-area farmers have shipped countless tons of rice around the world in times of war and peace. The local high schools have very active chapters of the Future Farmers of America.

An H-E-B location not far away has Tesla superchargers. Nearby "attractions" include the "Boot Barn," which of course features western footwear.

The Katy Buc-ee's location is also near a congregation of Asian cuisine restaurants, especially Chinese, Vietnamese, and Korean eateries. In between Katy and downtown Houston lies the "Energy Corridor," a stretch of I-10 featuring offices and headquarters for world players in the oil and oil-drilling market, such as Diamond Offshore drilling.

Old and new, in and around Katy, Texas. A theme which resonates throughout Texas.

Lake Jackson, Texas. Three locations:

Lake Jackson is the birthplace of Buc-ee's. To learn what Buc-ee's is all about, it's probably good to study this area south of Houston. This is where the West meets the South, the sea meets the prairie. Lake Jackson locations include:

- 899 Oyster Creek Drive

- 101 N Highway 2004

- 598 Highway 332

As you might expect, the Lake Jackson locations are not the gigantic "travel center" locations. Lake Jackson is about 45 miles southwest of the seaside city of Galveston.

Some points of interest near the Oyster Creek Drive location include:

- Phat Boyz restaurant, featuring Mexican cuisine. The restaurant is along Brazosport Boulevard, about two miles away.

- The nearby city of Clute. Construction workers discovered a fossilized mammoth here in the early 2000s. The city of Clute features a small museum with information about mammoths and about other fossils.

League City, Texas:

The League City Buc-ee's is:

- Located at 1702 League City Parkway.

- About 17 miles southeast of Houston's William P. Hobby Airport.

- About 25 miles northwest of the seaside resort of Galveston, Texas.

This location is a convenient stop in between Houston and the beaches around Galveston.

League City is named after an early settler, J.C. League. The city is one of the larger suburbs of the metro Houston area, with a population of over 110,000 residents.

Luling, Texas:

Now we are getting quite a bit afield from the metro Houston area.

The Luling store is about:

- 55 miles south of downtown Austin, Texas.

- 165 miles west of Houston, Texas.

- 80 miles northeast of San Antonio, Texas.

The Luling store is along Interstate 10, near the intersection of South Magnolia Avenue. Interesting to note that Buc-ee's has locations along I-10 ranging from the central Texas area (Luling) nearly to Florida (the Robertsdale, Alabama location).

Madisonville, Texas:

The Madisonville store is along Interstate 45, near the intersection of State Highway 21 West. This location is one of the few stores which is in the zone quite a distance between both the metro Houston area and the Dallas-Fort Worth Area.

The Madisonville location does include adjacent Tesla superchargers for Tesla vehicles — and for Ford electric vehicles beginning in the year 2024.

The Madisonville store is about:

- 95 miles north northwest of downtown Houston.

- 135 miles south of downtown Dallas.

- 100 miles southeast of Waco, Texas.

You're probably ready for a rest stop if you're at least 95 miles from any decent-sized city, especially if you're traveling from one of those cities. It appears it's fair to say that the Madisonville location is deep in the heart of Texas.

Interestingly named towns around Madisonville include "Flo" and "North Zulch."

Melissa, Texas:

This location is along I-75 near the intersection of... Buc-ee's Boulevard. Yes, some of the more recently built stores are along a street named "Buc-ee's." It's hard to argue with this trend, noting that in some cases the street was built mainly to allow access to the respective Buc-ee's locations.

The Melissa location:

- Has an address of 1550 Central Texas Expressway.

- Is about 35 miles north northeast of downtown Dallas, Texas.

- Is about 20 miles northeast of the massive Pepsi Frito-Lay facility in Plano, Texas.

- Has Tesla superchargers.

Folks who grew up in the 1970s, when thinking about Melissa, Texas, might be reminded of the song *Melissa,* by the Allman Brothers band. Fun fact: the title of the Allman Brothers song has an all-night grocery or "mini-mart" connection. Gregg Allman was having trouble thinking of "just the right" three-syllable woman's name for a song he was writing. One night he was in a Florida all-night grocery and a woman yelled out to her daughter "Melissa." According to a Wikipedia article, this name clicked with Gregg, and he soon finished the song.

New Braunfels, Texas: This location is one of the closest stores to San Antonio, Texas. The New Braunfels location is:

- About 30 miles northeast of downtown San Antonio.

- About 45 miles southwest of Austin, Texas.

• Was considered the largest convenience store in the world, until the Sevierville, Tennessee Buc-ee's location opened.

• One of the southwesternmost of Buc-ee's locations as of mid-2023. Most other locations are to the north in Texas, or are to the north and east in the "southeastern" U.S., or in the so-called "border states" of Kentucky and Tennessee.

Pearland, Texas. Two locations:

Well, if you're ever in the southern reaches of metro Houston, Texas, Buc-ee's has you covered. The Pearland locations are:

• 2541 South Main Street.

• 11151 Shadow Creek Parkway.

Pearland is:

• About 18 miles south of downtown Houston.

• Only about seven miles south of William P. Hobby Airport. Many consider Hobby Airport "just right" — not too small, not too big.

• About eight miles southeast of SaberCats stadium, the home field for the Houston SaberCats, a professional rugby team that competes in Major League Rugby. The league is considered one of the top levels of competition in North America. SaberCats stadium was built and completed in 2019 and has a capacity of 4,000 spectators.

A point of interest within a mile or two of the 2541 South Main Street Buc-ee's is:

● Central Texas Style BBQ joint, along "Broadway."

Port Lavaca, Texas:

The Port Lavaca store is:

● At 2318 West Main Street in Port Lavaca.

● About 120 miles southwest of Houston.

● About 140 miles southeast of San Antonio.

● About halfway between Houston and Corpus Christi, Texas, and is one of the southernmost Buc-ee's stores.

● About 240 miles north of Reynosa, Mexico, which is one of the nearest Mexican "border towns."

The Port Lavaca Buc-ee's store is near Lavaca Bay. The store is about two miles from Bayfront Peninsula Park and Port Lavaca Fishing Pier. Lavaca Bay connects with Matagorda Bay, which in turn connects with the Gulf of Mexico.

Richmond, Texas:

The Richmond location is about 25 miles south of central Houston. The Richmond store is:

- Along Interstate 69.

- At the address of 1243 Crabb River Road, near I-69.

- A few miles southwest of the large Houston suburb of Sugarland.

Royse City, Texas:

The Royse City store is about 30 miles northeast of central Dallas, Texas.

The Royse City location does feature Tesla Superchargers stations. Tesla recently announced its network will be open to Ford EV owners in 2024. And one day, you might be able to charge your Rolls Royce — in Royse City. (Rolls Royce recently announced plans to "roll out" an electric model.)

A nearby point of interest is Rockwall, Texas, which is about 10 miles southwest of Royse City. The city is named for a natural geologic feature — a naturally jointed series of sedimentary rock layers — which uncannily resembles a man-made structure or wall. This has given birth to all sorts of theories. Still, geologists say testing shows that the formations are natural sedimentation that has hardened into a layered appearance, which resembles a tile or even a brick wall of sorts.

Regarding Royse City, interestingly named nearby cities and towns include:

- Fate, Texas.

- Nevada, Texas.

- Poetry, Texas.

Temple, Texas:

The Temple store has an address of 4155 North General Bruce Drive.

The Temple store is:

- Along Interstate 35.

- About 75 miles north-northeast of Austin, Texas.

- In the category of Buc-ee's very large "Travel Centers."

- About 32 miles southwest of downtown Waco, Texas.

This is a fun geography question for readers. Buc-ee's recently expanded from Texas to Tennessee. If you want to move from Texas to Tennessee crossing only one state, which state is that? The answer (probably obvious for locals) will appear a few pages forward in the book. Read on!

Terrell, Texas:

The Terrell location is about 30 miles east of downtown Dallas, Texas. The Terrell store:

- Has an address of 506 West IH 20 (Interstate 20).

- Forms part of the ring of Buc-ee's locations surrounding downtown Dallas.

- Is a massive "Travel Center" location.

- Features Tesla superchargers.

Texas City, Texas:

The Texas City store has an address of 6201 Gulf Freeway (IH 45). It's a popular location between Houston and Galveston. A good spot to take a break while headed to — or from — the beach.

The Texas City store is not far from the "inland" shore of Galveston Bay, about ten to fifteen miles away.

Let's have some more fun with geography. Texas City is one of the relatively few cities in the country in which the city has the same name as the surrounding state. A partial list of other cities includes:

- Kansas City, Kansas. The much larger city of Kansas City, Missouri exists across the state line in Missouri. But, the state of Kansas also has a "Kansas City" — the third largest city in Kansas.

- New York, New York.

- Oklahoma City, Oklahoma.

Waller, Texas:

The Waller store is about 52 miles northwest of central Houston. The Waller location:

- Has an address of 40900 U.S. Highway 290 Bypass

- Is part of a string of Buc-ee's locations along Highway 290 stretching northwest from metro Houston. Other locations include Cypress and Giddings.

Some points of interest near the Waller Buc-ee's store give some local flavor. Points of interest nearby include:

- Waller County Line BBQ.

- Master Pumps and Power (an oilfield equipment distributor).

- Helena Chemical Company (an agrichemicals supplier).

Wharton, Texas:

The Wharton store:

- Has an address of 10484 U.S. 59 Road.

- Features Tesla superchargers.

- Has nearby points of interest such as Evelyn's Soulfood restaurant, which has an average rating on Google of 4.9 out of 5 stars. Evelyn's has quite a few Google reviews and features oxtail, fried chicken, mashed potatoes, and other dishes.

Well, that is it for all of the Buc-ee's locations as of June 2023. We will thus end it with the letter "W." Buc-ee's has not opened a location in Zulch, Texas — *NOT YET!*

It's been a thrill taking this tour of a *vast swath* of Americana while looking at Buc-ee's locations from Kentucky to South Texas. From Daytona to Dallas. We've covered a lot of ground. Thank you for enjoying the ride! Please leave a thumbs up and a comment. Suggestions are very welcome!

Question and answer to the "Tennessee" question from above:

Q.: If you want to move from Texas to Tennessee crossing only one state, which state is that? **Answer:** Arkansas.

This may be obvious for locals. Remember, not everyone is from Texas — though many want to be.

The End of *The Buc-ee's Phenomenon*

Thank you very much for reading **The Buc-ee's Phenomenon**. As Buc-ee's expands across the country, stay tuned for future editions covering the explosive growth — and fun — of Buc-ee's . — Timothy Fay

Additional books by Timothy Fay:

SUBURBAN DICTIONARY:

The Subtle, The Funny, And The Snarky:

Your Guide to Suburbanese

(Available at Amazon, Apple Books, Audible, Barnes & Noble, and all book outlets.)

Don't miss out!

Visit the website below and you can sign up to receive emails whenever Timothy Fay publishes a new book. There's no charge and no obligation.

https://books2read.com/r/B-A-CKSI-EPPOC

BOOKS2READ

Connecting independent readers to independent writers.